Select List of
British Parliamentary Papers
1955–1964

SOUTHAMPTON UNIVERSITY STUDIES
IN PARLIAMENTARY PAPERS

Select List of
British Parliamentary Papers
1955–1964

P. and G. FORD
and
DIANA MARSHALLSAY
Ford Collection of Parliamentary Papers
University of Southampton

IRISH UNIVERSITY PRESS
Shannon Ireland

© 1970

Irish University Press   Shannon   Ireland

SBN 7165 0884 2

Microfilm, microfiche and other forms of micro-publishing
© *Irish University Microforms   Shannon   Ireland*

Irish University Press   Shannon   Ireland
DUBLIN   CORK   BELFAST   LONDON   NEW YORK
T M MacGlinchey   Publisher

FILMSET AND PRINTED IN THE REPUBLIC OF IRELAND AT SHANNON
BY ROBERT HOGG PRINTER TO IRISH UNIVERSITY PRESS

CONTENTS

This volume contains

Sessional Papers from 1954–55 to 1963–64

Non-Parliamentary Publications from 1955 to 1964

In certain cases, papers issued after these dates are included when they are necessary to complete the account of investigations started within the period. References to earlier reports of enquiries completed in this period are given in the form of references to Breviate III, *A Breviate of Parliamentary Papers, 1940–1954,* by P. and G. Ford (1961).

ARRANGEMENT AND SCOPE OF THE VOLUME

In this Select List, as in that for the years 1833–1899 and the three volumes of Breviates, the papers are arranged in broad subject groups to show the development of parliamentary and government thinking in the various fields of policy. This enables the inquirer, to use Hansard's century-old words, 'to have before his eye the whole of any subject that has been treated on'. It does not attempt to reproduce the official indexes. With certain exceptions, it includes the reports and other material issued by committees, commissions and other bodies investigating economic, social and constitutional questions and matters of law and administration and the ensuing statements of government policy. Excluded by definition are papers dealing with foreign policy and with the constitutional status or internal policy of ex-colonial territories; it has, however, proved necessary to include some references to papers dealing with the economic and educational ties between this country and the Commonwealth, and with aid to developing countries generally. Also excluded are papers dealing with military and naval policy and with the organisation of the armed forces, but here again, because defence policy has repercussions on the economy in the field of manpower supply, finance, etc., a brief list of some of the relevant papers has been included. Information papers and technical reports and, in general, statistical publications have been excluded: the H.M.S.O. *Catalogues* should be consulted for these. Attempts to plan the economy as a whole require a great deal of statistical information: a brief guide to the sources of this material is included at the beginning of Section V.

It should be noted that there are two appendices: one gives the references to a select list of thirty of the most important annual reports; the other lists reports of various research series and of the Estimates Committee.

Readers should remember that the public corporations which run the various nationalised industries also act as their own publishers. Their annual reports are issued as Parliamentary Papers and some of their 'policy' documents (which are included in this Select List) are sold by H.M.S.O. and are therefore recorded in their *Catalogue*, but for the most part their publications will have to be sought in the *British National Bibliography*. This latter publication also lists, selectively, those government publications which are issued free (and which are not listed in the H.M.S.O. *Catalogue* because this is confined to sales items) and those which are sold direct to the public by the issuing department.

INTRODUCTION

As society grows and its needs alter, through its appropriate machinery it has to think not only of settling old problems but of making adjustments in its standards, practices and institutions to cope with new ones as they arise. These do not emerge in logical order and society has to turn its attention to them when and where the shoe pinches. Indeed, often only much later does historical hindsight reveal the deeper movements which were the origin or cause of the difficulties. The material in parliamentary papers enables one to feel the impact on society of some of these internal and external changes, to observe it working on the problems as they arise, now here, now there, to participate in its worries and thinking about them. This Select List is not, therefore, a finding list of titles set out in alphabetical or chronological order, but is arranged so that the reader, as he peruses its pages, can follow the development of inquiry and thought in the broad fields of public policy.

The List for the period has been particularly called for because the papers of these years—including in that term both the Sessional Papers and Non-Parliamentary or other government publications —are very voluminous and by reason of their number and varied origins present some difficulties to researchers. Their general form and titling follow the traditional pattern, which is fully described in the Introduction to the *Select List of British Parliamentary Papers, 1833–1899* and in the *Guide to Parliamentary Papers*. But there were some changes in the methods of inquiry.

First, although this Select List, like the Breviates and the Select List for the nineteenth century, aims at including policy papers, has the same scope and has been prepared on the same principles, there is a change of balance between the number of Parliamentary Papers arising in the House or presented by Command, bound in the sessional sets and included in the sessional indexes and those not arising in the House or presented, but issued through departments and which must be sought for outside the sessional papers and sessional indexes. In the Breviate for 1917–1939 there were rather less than four Parliamentary Papers to one Non-Parliamentary; in that for the fifteen years 1940–1954 the ratio was about three to two. In this List, covering the ten years 1955–1964, there are just under fourteen hundred papers, the Non-Parliamentary ones amounting to well over six hundred, thus getting within sight of equal numbers. These differences are far too great to be accounted for by any marginally more generous interpretation of the

1

definition used for deciding on inclusion. They represent a shift in the agencies and methods used for investigation. This great upsurge of inquiry was undertaken not only by the older types of bodies, the select committees, royal commissions and departmental committees, or by the innovation of the 'working party', used particularly to report on the reorganisation of certain industries after the war, but now by working groups (e.g., *Traffic in Towns*), groups (*Transport Needs of Great Britain in the Next 20 Years*), advisory panels (*Land Use in the Highlands and Islands*), panels (*Road Pricing*), management groups (*Road Safety. The Slough Experiment*), study groups (*Work, Grading, Training of Hospital Engineers*) and so on. And some departments themselves began setting up their own internal research units. Some of these bodies were not very different from the departmental committee, which usually contained a number of experts, M.P.s and persons knowledgeable in public affairs, but they often came into being in a different way. Many ministries have standing advisory committees or councils very large in membership, e.g., Central Advisory Council for Education (England), standing advisory committees to the Minister of Health. And either on the Minister's initiative or perhaps the initiative of an advisory committee or council itself, a matter may be referred to it for report, and it will, in form at least, appoint a special group or committee to undertake the investigation, the results of which in due course it will transmit to the Minister. For example, in the case of the Buchanan Report on *Traffic in Towns*, the Minister provided a steering group whose job it was to give general help to the working group in the interpretation of its terms of reference and any facilities required. The paper on *Re-organisation of Local Government in Scotland* arose out of a conference between representatives of the associations of local authorities and the Minister. Here the steering committee consisted of representatives of the elected members, while the working group consisted of officials. The famous Beeching Report on the *Re-Shaping of British Railways* does not contain his name, nor is it signed by him. It was formally issued by the British Railways Board of which he was the chairman.

What differences did these changes of circumstance make to the material the investigating bodies offered to Parliament and the public for consideration? One concerns the nature of the evidence, another its availability to the contemporary public and to the historian. To answer these questions it is convenient to look at the methods of contemporary inquiry in some historical perspective. First, many of the dramatic investigations of the early nineteenth century into social conditions, so praised by Marx for their competence and freedom from partisanship, were made by the traditional method of question and answer, and the whole of the evidence was reported to the House by the select committees, together with the minutes of their proceedings, or presented to Parliament by

Command in the case of commissions, as in the inquiries into children's employment; an example in the eighties was the Lords' Committee on Sweating. Victims of the conditions, children or adults, gave personal evidence and we should certainly be poorer if it had not been reported verbatim. Not only did this give the reader a sense of immediacy, but the historian has at his disposal all the evidence as heard by the committee or commission. It is true that this process was open to the two criticisms levelled by Mrs. Webb against the Labour Commission: that there could be undue reliance on oral evidence where other and modern methods of investigation would be more fruitful; and that it could lead to the collection of an immense bulk of oral evidence both difficult to manage and expensive to print. This was clearly the case with the Royal Commission on Inland Waterways (1910) and the Royal Commission on Poor Laws (1909), of which Mrs. Webb was herself a member. Perhaps the outstanding example of the nineteenth century was the Labour Commission which Mrs. Webb criticised; yet one historian, Clapham, went out of his way to commend the amplitude and indexing of its voluminous evidence.

The great nineteenth-century inquiries often supplemented the oral evidence by a use of memoranda submitted by individual witnesses or even provided by civil servants; and there were special inquiries by individual investigators, such as those by the indefatigable Tremenheere, by Miss Collet on women's employment for the Labour Commission, while those by Jackson and Pringle, Steel-Maitland and Miss Squire for the Poor Law Commission of 1905–1909 were more important than much of the oral evidence. But in the period 1955–1964 the problems to be investigated were different and new methods of research had been developed; there was sometimes a change of balance between the use of the different types of evidence and in the character of the evidence itself. It is interesting to compare the thirty pages of appendices to the Macmillan Report on *Finance and Industry* (1931), with the three volumes of appendices, including important papers by the Bank of England, issued by the Radcliffe Committee on the *Working of the Monetary System*. The Royal Commission on the *Taxation of Profits and Income* made public a list of eighteen main questions on which they would be glad to receive evidence; they received statements or memoranda from four hundred individuals and bodies, and considered one hundred and twenty memoranda from the Board of Inland Revenue, but they took oral evidence only on some of them, partly because some of the ground they had to cover could not usefully be explored by formal examination of witnesses. The issues were complex and sometimes theoretical, and decisions taken depended on the weight to be given to certain assumptions or the balance of argument. They therefore also held informal sittings for private discussion. The panel on *Road Pricing* discussed thirty papers, mostly by their own members, though other persons were consulted, and the report is highly technical. In the Newsom Committee Report on *Half Our Future*, the chapter on education in the slums contains extracts from material which earlier would have been more fully worked over by the older method of question and answer. But it also contains important statistical material, while the Crowther Report on *15 to 18* has a whole volume devoted to a survey, much of it made by elaborate sampling methods. To determine what was the effect of the P.A.Y.E. system of income tax on incentives, the Royal Commission on *Taxation of Profits and Income* had a special statistical inquiry made for it by the Government Social Survey. The Albemarle Committee on the *Youth Service* was helped by an outside statistician to discover, among other matters, how much spending money was available to these young people. Some of the really decisive material considered by the Robbins Committee on *Higher Education* was an elaborate statistical inquiry by Moser. The difference between the report of the Commission on *Depression of Trade and Industry* (1886), which tried to account for the failure to maintain trade and employment, and that of the report on the *Growth of the Economy to 1966*, which was a piece of team research into the conditions needed to achieve an average four per cent growth, measures the distance which both theory and statistical method had travelled. Some of the material thus offered is not 'evidence' as that term is popularly understood, but has more the character of the results of research, and the reader finds himself pondering, not on witnesses' answers to questions, but on the design and execution of a statistical operation.

Next there is the question of the publication of the evidence. It is not quite a trite one. In the nineteenth century, where the matters under discussion covered wide geographical areas, these were investigated by assistant or divisional commissioners, as in the case of the Royal Commission on the *Poor. Laws* (1834), *Municipal Corporations* (1835), *Depressed Conditions of the Agricultural Interests* (1881–1882) and *Agricultural Depression* (1894–1897). This evidence was massive in bulk and very expensive to produce, but whatever its contemporary value, is now being worked over again by historians. The evidence taken by select committees is reported to the House and ordered to be printed, while that of royal commissions is issued in the Command or Non-Parliamentary series. In the present period, however, there were a large number of departmental and advisory committees, groups, etc., many on minor matters but some on important ones, whose reports describe, quote from and assess the evidence, oral and written, and list the persons or bodies who offered it; but it is not printed. A glance at this List will certainly show how massive and expensive the undertaking to print would be. Fortunately, the standards of reporting and investigation are high, but it does mean that the historian can touch the evidence only at one remove.

In some of these major inquiries there is the old problem of whether the evidence is to be found in the sessional papers and listed in their indexes or in the Non-Parliamentary papers. The Royal Commission on *Taxation of Profits and Income* presented its report as a Command paper, but its evidence is Non-Parliamentary. The vital inquiry into the *Working of the Monetary System* was made by a committee. Its report is a Command paper, its evidence, including important papers by the Bank of England, was issued as Non-Parliamentary papers, in this following the precedent of the equally famous Macmillan Report on *Finance and Industry*. On the other hand, the investigation into *Higher Education* was made by a committee (Ld Robbins, chairman) which published all its evidence as Command papers, but the Franks inquiry into *Administrative Tribunals* was also by a committee and its evidence was issued as Non-Parliamentary papers.

In the period covered by this List, 1955–1964, governments and the community had inherited from the activities of the previous decade and were concerned with definite commitments on several matters of public policy. First, the organisation of the fuel and power industries and the railways on the basis of national ownership; secondly, a scheme of social security which embodied the work of a whole generation of experts, administrators, doctors and voluntary workers, and covered not only payments during unemployment and sickness, but a national health service; thirdly, through the Education Act, 1944, to a great reorganisation of education, the provision of schools and teachers, a widened approach, the opening of full opportunities for children to reach all levels of education up to the highest. Fourthly, and in some ways the most important of all, there was a deep commitment to the maintenance of full employment which the investigations of the inter-war years, now galvanised by Keynesian theory, had apparently made possible. To this was now added a new objective, that of accelerating economic growth to a specified target annual rate. It is in the light of these activities that the character of the papers in these years is best seen. The particular statutes which commence great social and political experiments are but the formal launching of the ships. They then have to prove themselves in the open seas, with their chances of storm and currents. That is what many of the papers of this period are about.

When the Labour government of 1945 decided to carry through by a process of nationalisation, those unifications of the coal, gas and electricity supply industries and of the railways which had been foreshadowed as far back as the 'Reconstruction' reports of 1917–1919, in order to avoid the dangers of Parliamentary, ministerial, and bureaucratic meddling with their management, instead of placing them under direct Parliamentary control it created independent commissions and boards. These were to have full power to work on business principles, provided that the industries were made to pay one year with another, that they obtained consent for capital borrowing and some assent for general price policy, and presented an annual report. When ideas of nationalisation of coal mining and of railways began to find their way into significant political programmes, say after 1906, it was regarded as a means of greatly improving efficiency, output and conditions of employment; and although there were already warning signs, even in the reconstruction plans after 1918 it had not been fully envisaged that they might become declining industries, with contraction rather than expansion ahead of them. But the competition with coal of rival fuels—oil and atomic energy—and of motor transport with railways, meant that many hopeful expectations were disappointed, that these two industries now faced substantial contraction, that millions had to be wiped off their debts, that *Plan for Coal* (1950) was a failure and *Investing in Coal* (1956) in jeopardy. Quite irrespective of M.P.s' tendency to meddle, it was clear that Parliament would not in these circumstances be passively content with the 'constitutional' arrangements for remote supervision of economic policy pursued by industries so basic to the economy. Many papers on these nationalised industries deal with these two problems.

On the first, in line with the original ideas about the independence of the commissions and boards, the Select Committee on *Nationalised Industries* was to obtain information on current policies and practices, but excluded from its scope were matters within the responsibility of the Minister, questions of wages, etc., subject to collective bargaining arrangements, matters which had to be considered by some formal statutory machinery and questions of day-to-day administration. But from this position the committee advanced step by step into a new field of 'constitutional' arrangements. By 1958–59 it considered the general problem of the link of these industries with the House, wanted the services of an accountant and an economist and other research staff who, in order to preserve the independence of the Committee, were to be the servants of Parliament and not of the executive—a development which departments must have regarded with doubts as a rival and duplicating their duty. But the Committee was not to interfere with the working of the nationalised industries, whose co-operation was to be assured by the security applied to the confidential information they supplied. By 1959–60, when the British Transport Commission preserved its formal independence by itself inviting the select committee to make an investigation, the Committee was not afraid to make what must have been a burdensome investigation lasting six months at a time when the Commission was engaged in reorganisation and when a non-planning board was set up for the

Government's own purpose covering the same ground. There were tricky questions involved. The Treasury's concern was the level of these industries' investment plans because the national interest was involved and public money was at stake. On the other hand, while the Minister would have to consider the national interest, the British Transport Commission did not always consult him because it had a statutory duty to have regard to the needs of the public, agriculture, industry and commerce. And in 1961–62 the Committee, reviewing the outcome of the recommendations and conclusions of former committees, declared that it was satisfied that to a substantial extent they had been carried out and that such investigations were useful from time to time.

The second set of problems, the economic policy and management of the separate industries—coal, electricity, gas, railways and air transport—was complicated by the fact that nationalisation itself introduced some conflict of approach. Were they to make decisions according to what was economically right or what was socially desirable? For this reason, the principle that they should in general pay their way and be run on commercial lines was not always easy of application. The Minister agreed that the Electricity Area Boards should not be required to consult him as well as consultative councils and the Electricity Council before fixing their charges, as this would hamper the exercise of their commercial responsibility. But there were informal arrangements which enabled the Gas Boards to ascertain the Minister's view before varying the level of their prices and the Boards were apparently expected to give weight to national interests. The White Paper on the *Financial and Economic Obligations of the Nationalised Industries* reviewing the experience of ten years, was still a little uncertain. They should aim at efficiency with a maximum contribution to 'economic well-being', and though adjustments should be made for any non-commercial obligations imposed on them from outside, they were not to be regarded as social services absolved from economic and commercial justification. While the return to private capital over the previous five years was round about fifteen per cent, public concerns, though not strictly comparable, earned considerably less than five per cent; and this difference might imply over-investment in public concerns and artificial stimulation of demand for their products by public pressure for unduly low prices.

The efforts of the industries to meet these different criteria included changes in structure, organisation and pricing policy, and the papers show how much work was done on them. In the declining industries, coal mining and railways, these problems were especially acute; and in addition to cancellations of debt and steps to cushion them against competition, through a variety of bodies there were repeated endeavours to find satisfactory solutions.

Sometimes suggestions came from the industries themselves, as in the Coal Board's *Plan for Coal* (1950), *Investment in Coal* (1956) and the British Waterways Board's *Future of the Waterways* (1964). The British Transport Commission put forward, in accordance with statute, the *Railways Re-Organisation Scheme* transferring departmental authority to the regions, as it did in the plan for the *Modernisation and Re-equipment of British Railways* and the *Proposals for the Railways*; but the later plan to break up the cumbersome structure of the Transport Commission created to co-ordinate the whole of the transport undertakings—railways, ports, inland waterways and London transport—and to place each of these activities under a separate board, came from the Government in a White Paper on the *Re-organisation of the Nationalised Transport Undertakings*. The attempt to foresee the *Transport Needs of Great Britain in the Next Twenty Years* was made by a Ministry of Transport working group. The experience of outside business was drawn upon in the Fleck Report on the *Organisation* of the National Coal Board, the Herbert Report on the *Electricity Supply Industry* and in the most famous of all, the Beeching Report on *Re-shaping of British Railways*, whose proposals to shed a large range of losing branches and services and to create a smaller, highly efficient and viable system using revolutionary methods of working, met with strong opposition from local communities and vested interests and from the railway unions moved by fear of redundancies and a smaller field of employment.

Of the tasks of the second commitment, the most difficult arose from the establishment of the National Health Service. After seven years' working it was due for a scrutiny: the mere rise of the cost to public funds from £340 million a year to £440 million ensured that. But how much of this increase was due simply to the rise of prices, how much to an actual increase in the use of real resources, both in total and per head of the population likely to use it? Did this expenditure produce an 'adequate' service, and what was the meaning of 'adequate'? Since the Government through the Health Service largely determined the demand for doctors and the medical schools their supply, was the number of doctors in the service about right, deficient, or excessive? What principles of remuneration were needed to secure the right recruitment? Newsholme and others in 1909 argued strongly for the unification of the curative and the preventive health services, the Dawson of Penn Report on the *Future Provision of Medical and Allied Services* (1920) for planned provision of general hospitals largely conducted by general practitioners, and for a single health authority in each district to supervise local authorities' and all the allied services, curative and preventive. In fact, the National Health Insurance Scheme and the National Health Service following it, in some ways accepted the tripartite division between municipal services, hospital and general practitioner services, but many problems had remained unsolved. Should these now be unified or adjusted, by the transfer of hospitals to the local authorities, or of the whole health services from the Minister to a national health corporation? Could we now replace the rather haphazard location of hospitals, etc., by planned provision? The political din raised by the attempts to dampen down the great rise of expenditure on prescriptions by the imposition of charges raised questions of principle which went beyond the sums involved. Was the rise due to an elastic demand when prices are reduced to zero, or was it the result of meeting real needs which had hitherto been untreated? Was it due to the doctors' use of expensive proprietary drugs, possibly influenced by high-pressure selling by the manufacturers, or to real, if expensive, advances in medical knowledge? If the doctor were to feel free to give the treatment he thought right, what was meant by 'over-prescribing'? Many inquiries were made into these questions, the most comprehensive and penetrating being that by the Guillebaud Committee on the *Cost of the National Health Service*; there were three papers on prescribing, five on general plans for the provision of hospitals, four dealing with the number of doctors and their pay, while a very large number endeavoured to pool the experience of the service as a whole on many matters of administration.

The third commitment arose from the White Paper on *Educational Reconstruction*, 1943, and the Education Act, 1944, implementing it, which aimed at reorganising primary education up to the age of eleven plus, raising the school leaving age by stages to fifteen and then to sixteen, expanding the facilities for further education up to eighteen, including provision for part-time day release, and providing easier access to the universities. The McNair, Fleming and Norwood Committees (1943–1944) had examined the subsidiary questions of the ways and means of securing the requisite supply of teachers, the place of the public schools and the content of education itself. Great progress was made in most of these fields in numbers, buildings, training of teachers, but it was not surprising that after a decade the whole problem should be looked at again in the light of experience and changing ideals. From the beginning of the nineteenth century questions of education have stimulated many and elaborate inquiries which bulk largely in the total. This arises partly from the care for children, partly because questions of values are involved. In few areas of policy do changes in the ideas of what is requisite for political and social democracy or the immediate needs of society show themselves more insistently, or arouse such discussion. Psychological knowledge of and the assumptions about children alter, expansion involves providing public money on a large scale and working through locally elected statutory bodies. The long list of inquiries shows that this period is no exception and indicates once again the enthusiasm and work with which these developments were pursued by various bodies. It is, indeed, significant that many topics reported on in the period 1943 to 1950 and even after World War I were gone into again and that there was even some repetitiveness in title. It is interesting to note what was new, what was reaffirmed, what changes new knowledge and alterations of social feeling had wrought. Was the age of eleven plus the proper age psychologically and socially at which to determine the selection of children for the different types of post-primary education? Should the schools be co-educational, comprehensive? And what should the content of that education be? On this the White Papers on *Secondary Education for All* and *Education in Scotland; the Next Step* have something to say. The work of the Crowther Committee *15 to 18* was overlapped by that of other bodies on future demand for teachers, by the Carr subcommittee of the National Joint Advisory Council to the Ministry of Labour on *Training for Skill*, by the Lord de la Warr Committee on *Further Education in Agriculture*, the McMeeking Committee on *Art Education* and the Anderson Committee on *Grants to Students*. There were White Papers on *Technical Education*, on *Better Opportunities for Technical Education* and a report by H.M. Inspectors of Education on *Forward from School; the Links between School and Further Education*; reports on how to fit into the scheme *Maladjusted Children* (Underwood), by the Newsom Committee on *Half Our Future*, i.e., on children of average or less than average ability; and on provision for the leisure of children and young people by the Albemarle Committee on the *Youth Service in England and Wales*, since the problems of the restiveness of these young people, the changed relations of the family and some decline in religious influences were already showing themselves. And the List shows many inquiries into the application of these principles in Scotland and Wales, on the adjustment of curriculum, examinations, and so on. And the final stage was taken up again by the Robbins Committee on *Higher Education*.

The papers concerning the fourth commitment, full employment and economic growth, have a unity and significance which were new. When the reformers of other decades, such as the Benthamites of the early nineteenth and the radical reformers in the early twentieth century, endeavoured to introduce into legislation new political and social principles, they were able to apply them to this or that separate problem as urgency and political circumstances made it desirable and practicable, knowing that success in any field would not be endangered because other fields were yet untouched. Any feeling of unity in papers about them came less from the interconnectedness of the problems they dealt with, than from the principles being applied. But full employment and economic growth are inter-related, many of the factors concerned—savings, investment, prices, supply of money, the foreign balance—not only reacting on one another, but being in a sense quantitatively inter-locked. The significance of any paper often lies not only in the specific problem it deals with, but in its relation to others. In this field, however, many important day-to-day, short-run measures of policy taken in pursuance of these aims, e.g., changes in the Bank Rate, restrictions on hire purchase, changes of taxation, were not the outcome of formal inquiry but of ministerial decisions an-nounced in the House and elsewhere.

The commitment to full employment was more easily fulfilled, by and large, than we had a right to expect. There was an element of trial and error, of hit and miss, and in practice we had much to learn. The components of the Keynesian theory—national income, saving, investment, propensity to consume, the foreign balance—were concepts of aggregates, each resulting from the activities of in-dividuals and groups. They were not easy to forecast in amount or in the form most useful for policy, and knowledge of the functional relations between them was still limited. The early attempts to counter over-expansion or over-depression by reducing or in-creasing spending showed that these measures did not act quickly enough and that the instruments of monetary policy were not always well understood. The requirements which Beveridge had laid down in his *Full Employment in a Free Society*, that employers should not meet increased demand by restrictive practices, nor unions make competitive wage demands, were not fully met. In practice what happened was that whenever employment seemed likely to get out of hand either way, ministers rather pragmatically and not always with theoretical consistency, picked what seemed to be the appropriate instrument at the time to check the movement. Nevertheless, as compared with a level of unemployment varying between 10 per cent and 22 per cent in the inter-war years and of $8\frac{1}{2}$ per cent in Beveridge's social security plan, it was now usually below his later estimate of 3 per cent.

This success brought up the whole question of economic growth. For when output and standards of living had been raised by bringing idle workers and resources into full employment, it was only from economic growth that further improvements could come. But it also engendered the hope not only that we could speed this up, but by deliberate management of the economy it could be made to grow at some given average rate per annum. This con-viction was something quite new. For in the period of reform 1906–1914, the general body of the people, though looking forward to rising standards, would not have dreamed of expecting, or political leaders of promising anything so definite. But in 1954 Mr. R. A. Butler dramatically woke up the *Invest in Success* Con-servative Conference at Blackpool by repeating a point he had made earlier to the National Joint Production Advisory Committee, that we could aim at doubling the standard of life in twenty-five years. This hope was repeated in the Conservative Manifesto of 1955. In 1959 Mr. Gaitskell thought that his programme of social improvements might be met without the pains of increased taxation (except capital gains tax) out of the results of economic growth. All this gave a new twist to parties' political discussions and has not since been allowed to drop out of party aims and promises.

This implied a distinction between potential output and actual output, between 'natural growth' and 'full natural growth', and an examination of the ways in which the gaps between them might be closed. There was much to learn on what steps to take, and when to take them and of what magnitude they should be. The task was to identify the various operative factors, to work the facts of experience, ideas, hints and bits of argument into some kind of reasonable theory coherent enough for practical purposes. Rates of growth have varied over time in individual countries, e.g., in the United Kingdom, and been uneven as between different areas in the same country, some growing fast, others slowly, but rarely without change of speed. Sometimes the growth has been led by a special advance in some one industry whose development has had repercussions on the whole balance of the industrial structure. Then some notions were required of the relation of the quantities of input of man-power, capital, and in a sense of technology, to output or income per head. Traditional theory had given most attention to the problems arising from the allocation of given resources to different uses, but Keynes examined the conditions of variations of output as a whole. His theory was a short-run theory, particularly apt for the special case of the British economy in the inter-war years, with its mass unemployment. But it was static, assumed many factors fixed and did not tell us much about the long-run path of development. Active exploration by economists of the theoretical problems of macro-economics (even though the results were sometimes expressed in abstract mathematical terms and seemed remote from the actual issues of policy) increased the awareness of what might be involved. The papers were more and more influenced by these ideas. As the functional relationships of the various components of growth were more fully understood it became possible, not only to pick out and endeavour to reduce or remove the various obstacles to growth, but to advance step by step to co-ordinating policies into a general plan or target.

War experience had shown that the mere attempt to make an overall plan reveals possible bottlenecks of particular kinds of skill or specified types of production, such as machine tools. Interest in the problem of population shifted to its man-power aspects, the possible shortage of scientific and technological man-power and its effective use (seven papers) as well as to replacing declining forms of industrial training by those more suitable for an age of automation (two papers). For contrived growth we could no longer rely on spontaneous invention stimulated by the patent system; it must be more organised and given government guidance and support (six papers). And one of our weaknesses, the long time-lag between discovery and application, could be shortened by spending more on development. Growth rates could be increased by setting out to stimulate and reorganise key, lagging industries, such as machine tools, building construction, shipbuilding, and by the diversion of industrial development from prosperous areas in the south-east in which expansion might be complicated by labour shortages to areas where it was lagging and the resources of labour not fully used, as in the north-east, mid-Wales, Scotland and Northern Ireland, thus commencing self-sustaining growth (seven papers). Restrictive practices whether by trade unions on the use of labour (one paper) or by business firms which have the effect of raising costs, prices and the loss of socially desirable output (reports of the Monopolies and Restrictive Practices Commission) were out of place in an expanding economy. Two major questions of policy had the same objective; the creation of a wider international market either in the European Free Trade Association or in the European Economic Community would lead to cost reductions, specialisation and expansion of trade of its members (eleven papers). By 1963 many of these particular studies were drawn together in the reports on the *Growth of the Economy to 1966* and on *Conditions Favourable to Faster Growth*, presented to the National Development Council set up in 1962, which accepted that a target of overall growth of four per cent per annum between 1961 and 1966 could be attained without undue strain.

In economic matters English society was thus pursuing not just one, but several objectives, not all of which were completely compatible or, save in most exceptional circumstances, capable of achievement at the same time in equal degree: full employment, economic growth, stabilisation of prices, safe-guarding exchange rates and the balance of payments. And the emphasis given to one or the other at any time depended not only on changes in external economic conditions, but on the varying pressures of political parties, groups and interests. The endeavour to bring employment up to and maintain it near full employment led to a steady, creeping inflation. Half the £4,000 million increase in the value of our production in 1952–1956 was due not to a rise in output in real terms but to a money rise owing to inflation of prices and costs. The expansion provided opportunities for trade unions (and not only those of manual workers) to compete in wage bargaining without reference to the general situation, thus contributing to a wage-cost spiral. This competitive element arose partly from the stress on 'comparability' between industries, as evidenced by the Guillebaud Report on *Railway Pay* (Special Joint Committee on Machinery of Negotiation for Railway Staff, 1960), that of the Pilkington

Commission on *Doctors' and Dentists' Remuneration* (1959–60), the setting up of the Civil Service Pay Research Unit, following the Priestley Commission (1955), though the Willink Commission on *Police* and Jewkes' minority report in the Pilkington inquiry criticised this practice, and the insistence on maintaining differentials between grades. Indeed, workers seemed to be keeping as close an eye on the pay of the man on the next bench, in the next workshop and in the office as on profits.

It was the ambiguity of aim which hampered the efforts to deal with this situation which the papers record. The Council on *Prices, Productivity, and Incomes* (the three 'wise men') set up in 1957 to watch these relations in the hope that its reports would influence the policies of those concerned, was to have regard to the desirability of full employment, economic growth and stable prices. The burden of its four reports was that money incomes had risen substantially faster than real productivity, that this inflation was inimical to growth, and that this result was a 'common responsibility'. The White Paper on *Incomes Policy: The Next Step* (1962) setting out the principles of voluntary restraint, included suggestions that wage increases should not normally exceed two per cent to two and a half per cent, and that less attention should be paid to 'comparability'. The National Incomes Commission was required, when dealing with wage agreements referred to them because these principles seemed not to have been borne in mind, to have regard to the desirability of keeping the increase of aggregate money incomes within the long-run rates of increase of national production (five papers). But the problem was one not merely of a clash of theory, but of antagonism of interest: the T.U.C. would not participate in or support any of these inquiries. The rise of costs seemed also to threaten the balance of payments and the stability of the exchange rates. Repeated pulses of expansion and checks, 'stop and go', did not provide the best atmosphere for growth. Control of the economy by the manipulation of the Bank Rate, which seemed easy at the time of the Macmillan Committee on *Finance and Industry* (1931) in the depth of deflation, was not so effective when a large part of capital investment in fuel, power and transport was in the public sector and not sensitive to alterations of the rate of interest or when there had been many changes in the structure and working of the monetary system. When governments aimed at these different objectives, giving more emphasis now to one, now to the other, views of the efficacy of monetary policy generally had to become a little more modest and its various techniques more sophisticated. This it was the task of the Radcliffe Committee to unravel, in an exhaustive report, after considering voluminous evidence. Though the circumstances in which it was produced were not so dramatic as those when the Macmillan Committee reported and the aim of reducing mass unemployment over-shadowed all others, it remains one of our great state papers, for it shows how many things we had to learn for the next stage, that of controlling the economy as a whole.

General economic development as well as government policy called for some reshaping of the machinery of Government and of the processes of administration. These included, for example, several and occasionally repeated transfers of functions between the ministries, carried out under the Ministers of the Crown (Transfer of Functions) Act, 1947, the internal organisation of the Treasury to separate its economic and financial work from that concerning the conduct of the Civil Service and the personal link of its head with the Cabinet Secretariat, and the establishment of the National Economic Development Council. Many of these, set out in detail in *The Organisation of British Central Government, 1914–64* (2nd ed. by F. M. G. Willson, Allen & Unwin, 1968) were the result of government decision rather than the outcome of formal inquiry. But in three areas there were important papers.

First, the great extensions of the social services and deliberate government control of the economy required for their operation either detailed regulations and decisions affecting individuals, such as their rights to unemployment benefit, or quasi-judicial, administrative decisions needed to carry out policy, such as restrictions on individuals' use of their own land or its acquisition by public authorities, and thus raised once again questions of the balance of administrative convenience and individual liberty which had been reported on by the Donoughmore Committee on *Ministers' Powers* (1933). That committee was concerned with the threat to Parliamentary sovereignty by Ministers' powers to make regulations outside the purview of the Courts and to take decisions affecting individuals from which they had no appeal, with securing the subjection of all classes and bodies to the law, with the liberty of the individual and his unimpeded access to the means of remedy. But the field of such decisions had expanded over a very wide front. Each year there were 50,000 decisions on national insurance cases; rent tribunals produced another 15,000; town and country planning 6,000; and the National Health Service gave patients a right of complaint against doctors. Partly as a result of the Crichel Down case, the aspect of the problem which now received most attention from the Franks Committee on *Administrative Tribunals and Enquiries* (1957) was the protection of the individual; proceedings should be open, fair and impartial, and detailed procedures were recommended to that end. The 2,000 tribunals of various kinds were to be supervised by a Council on Tribunals (England and Wales) with a Scottish committee. But one fundamental principle of policy was reaffirmed. Like the Donoughmore Committee, it rejected the proposals for a system of administrative law and an over-riding administrative court.

Nor had the machinery of local government caught up with the new facts, either with the great shifts of population, whether due to town populations pushing their way into surrounding rural areas or the result of state policy on the regional redistribution of industry, with the increased disparities in size and resources of the different types of authority, or with the imposition on them of a wide range of new duties which, since some authorities were weak, also involved more central control. Its organisation had remained substantially unchanged since 1888 and 1894. The first systematic effort to put things right had come to nothing. The Eve Commission, directed to adjust local government boundaries, had concluded in 1947 that this was not possible without considering functions, and had proposed far-reaching changes. But these were not accepted. In the meantime, the conditions of solution had been affected by another factor, the five Associations of municipal corporations, county councils, urban district councils, rural district councils and parish councils which, though non-party political and voluntary, were powerful because of their experience and because the success of any scheme of reorganisation depended on their co-operation. But they failed to agree among themselves, and when the Minister rejected the proposal of the Association of Municipal Corporations to extend the one-tier system, and that of the other Associations for a spread of the two-tier system, there was left the compromise set out in the White Paper on the *Areas and Status of Local Authorities in England and Wales*, to appoint two commissions, one for England and one for Wales, to make proposals for changes on specific matters, leaving the main principles of organisation intact. The main problem was thus carried forward.

This lag of local constitutional reform was most serious in the case of the six great conurbations, in each of which the responsibility for the services for their large populations was divided between a number of authorities, some autonomous county boroughs, others part of a two-tier county system. It was acute in the case of London whose problems, difficult anyway, were made nearly insoluble by out-moded machinery. Pressing as the difficulties were, here also the first effort had failed, for none of the 1923 Ullswater Commission's conclusions were then acted on, though a minority report by Donald and Walsh had pointed the way to a directly-elected Greater London Council, and one by Hiley and Talbot to the division of London into one-tier county boroughs. Here also conflicts of interest between different parts of the region, between different types of authority and of political philosophy meant a delay of thirty-five years. In the meantime, difficulties had accumulated as the problem had grown more urgent and as the evidence given at the Herbert Commission shows, there were some interesting changes of view on the part of the local bodies and even of political parties. This Commission was thus able to cut through the

tangle of interests and difficulties and to come to unanimous conclusions which were in some ways a reversal of what had earlier
been the effective trend of thinking. In effect, instead of the existing
two-tier system they proposed to make the new boroughs primary
authorities having enlarged duties, with a directly-elected Greater
London Council to take on specific functions appropriate to the
region.

The immense amount of material in the papers was not gathered
for the use of historians, but provided to aid contemporary policy-
making. Even the M.P. most industrious at his homework would
not be able to master more than a fraction of it. The story of the
varied fortunes of the reports would be out of place here, but the
papers themselves tell something about the processes of their trans-
lation into action. Some were followed by White Papers setting out
the Government's considered policy. Others supplied proposals
and supporting argument, out of which a minister and his civil
service advisors could by acceptance, modification or rejection,
shape a practical policy, or which some of the many interested
groups within or without the political parties could support, push
or oppose. In certain cases proposals, though arrived at after
detailed or laborious investigation, were broad and clear enough
for a great part of the electorate or at least the most active part of
it, to understand and consider, as in the case of those on *Local
Government in Greater London*, mental health or some questions of
education. But effective understanding of the Radcliffe Committee
Report on the *Working of the Monetary System* required close,
practical acquaintance with business and finance or expertise much
beyond the powers of the mass of the electorate, or even of some
backbench Members, who would have to look to the lead of the
small, knowledgeable group within their own party.

Then the plurality of objectives and multiplicity of interests
touched by the endeavours to control the economy as a whole were
bound to lead to demands of groups for consultation and representa-
tion, to pressures by unions and by the City, by doctors in the health
and teachers in the education services about pay and status, by
railway unions about the pace of modernisation. And the fate of the
Beeching Report shows how strong such group resistance could be.
The policy of diverting industry to less prosperous regions led not
only to detached assessment of their prospects, but to some competitive pressures from the different regions for government aid
and support. How much heed should a government give to associations of local authorities over the reform of the structure of local
government on the ground that they represented the wishes of local
electors, if it were also argued that they represented particular forms
of local authority in danger of obsolescence? Attempts to separate
technical from political issues in incomes policy by setting up
independent bodies, the Council on Prices, Productivity and

Incomes and the National Incomes Commission, were not successful because powerful groups, trade unions, were hostile. On the other hand, outside the economic field, various groups within and without the political parties played a more creative role. The papers throw some incidental light on whether these group pressures are more released and stronger when electoral opinion is evenly divided and the parties are competing keenly for support, and on what is their effect when parties have a strong political doctrine.

Though the three political parties accepted the main economic targets, full employment, economic growth, a proper balance of payments and the stabilisation of prices and though on these matters there might be differences of emphasis and in choice of technique, the economic circumstances left them with only modest room for individual manoeuvre. Any wandering too far afield by the parties in pursuit of their own political programmes might be checked by the insistent realities of the balance of payments— penalties which both parties experienced. It was rather in the broad margins round the central economic problem and in the areas of social policy outside it that the differences of party policy showed themselves. On some matters the party machines had already formulated their approach through their own methods and in the light of their own traditional political philosophies: in the economic field, emphasis on private enterprise, more opportunity, diminution of tax dis-incentives and selective social security payments on the one hand, nationalised enterprise, greater equality and taxation of socially created wealth on the other. Their immediate programmes so arrived at were set out in their election statements: *Forward with Labour* (1955), *Members One of Another* (1959), *The New Britain* (1964) by the Labour Party; *United for Peace* (1955), *The Use of Leisure* (1959), *Prosperity with a Purpose* (1964) by the Conservative Party; *Thinking for Yourself* (1964) by the Liberal Party. Thus it came about that iron and steel and some road transport had been nationalised, then de-nationalised, and iron and steel re-nationalised, while the nationalisation of coal mining, railways and electrical power was left untouched.

Yet throughout this period the electorate was so closely and stubbornly divided in opinion that there was never more than a five per cent difference in the total votes cast for the two main parties. In 1950 and 1951 it was so close that the majorities in the House were too small to be really workable, and the deadlock in this sense was broken in 1955 and 1959 because under the British electoral system small majorities in a large number of constituencies gave the successful party a large number of seats. This may have been due partly to the fact that the matters on which the electorate was asked to decide were not those of simple, broad political principle, but measures the success of which depended on complicated technical and economically inter-related matters not easily settled by popular vote. Indeed, public opinion tended to judge mainly by the evidence on particular topics such as wages, prices and housing, perhaps the balance of payments in a general way, and by the differences between promise and performance. At any rate, a substantial body of the electorate tended to keep within their traditional party loyalties.

Taken as a whole, the papers reflect the results of this interplay between analysis, economic urgencies, party and group pressures. Some problems, such as that of the press, remained obstinate, but in other fields—the penal system, prisons, treatment of young offenders, education, marriage and divorce—there was a forward movement and an increased understanding that the administrative machinery had to be adapted to new tasks. At the beginning of the period much work was done on tidying up and putting into good order some of the economic and social experiments commenced in the years following 1945. By its end the papers give a sense of a community which, despite the unresolved difficulties of its central economic problems and some confusion between the short-run and long-run measures needed to deal with conflicting objectives, was nevertheless trying to get ready for another comparable effort.

July 1970   P. Ford

ABBREVIATIONS

The following abbreviations have been used:

Adv.	Advisory
Agric.	Agriculture
ann.	annual
app.	appendix
Bd.	Board
Ch.	Chairman
Com.	Commission, Commissioners
C.S.O.	Central Statistical Office
Ct.	Court
Cttee.	Committee
Dept.	Department, Departmental
D.S.I.R.	Department of Scientific & Industrial Research
Educ.	Education
ev.	evidence
Fish.	Fisheries
Gen.	General
Govt.	Government
HL.	House of Lords
Inter-Dept.	Inter-Departmental
Jt.	Joint
Ld.	Lord
Memo.	Memorandum
Min.	Ministry
mins. of ev.	minutes of evidence
Nat.	National
N.E.D.C.	National Economic Development Council
N.I.	National Insurance
N.S.	National Service
proc.	proceedings
Rep.	Report
R.Com.	Royal Commission
Scot.	Scotland
Sel. Cttee.	Select Committee
U.G.C.	University Grants Committee

SUBJECT CLASSIFICATION OF PAPERS

page

I. MACHINERY OF GOVERNMENT

1. The Crown, Peerage

1955–56 Cmd.9483	xiii	Crown lands. Cttee. A. M. T. Eve, *Ch.* Rep.
1957 Non-Parl.		Crown Estate Com. Rep. (see succeeding Ann. Reps.).
1954–55 (HL.23)	iii	Wedgwood Benn (Renunciation) Bill. Personal Bills Cttee. Rep., proc., mins. of ev., etc.
1960–61 (142)	vi	Petition concerning Mr. Anthony Neil Wedgwood Benn. Privileges Cttee. R. A. Butler, *Ch.* Rep., proc., mins. of ev., apps.

2. Parliament

i. Elections

1962–63 (111)	vii	Parliamentary elections [Applications from members of H.M. Forces for release to become candidates]. Sel. Cttee. H. Brooke, *Ch.* 1st Rep.
(262)	vii	—— 2nd Rep., proc., mins. of ev., etc.

ii. Electoral Boundaries

1954–55 Cmd.9360	xiii	Electorates of local government areas in counties affected by the recommendations of the Boundary Commission for England. Statement. (see Breviate III, p. 5).

Boundary Com. for England. Reps.

1955–56 (227)	xi	—— Areas comprised in constituencies in the City of Nottingham; . . . Colchester, Maldon, Saffron Walden, etc. E. Simes, *Deputy Ch.*
1958–59 (255)	ix	—— Areas comprised in the constituencies of Ilford North; Ilford South, etc. K. Diplock, *Deputy Ch.*
1959–60 (60)	ix	—— Areas comprised in the constituencies of Walsall North; Walsall South, etc. K. Diplock, *Deputy Ch.*
1963–64 (25)	ix	—— Areas comprised in the constituencies of Eccles; Salford West, etc. G. A. Thesiger, *Deputy Ch.*

Boundary Com. for Scotland. Rep.

1959–60 (73)	ix	—— Areas comprised in the constituencies of West Fife and Dunfermline Burghs, etc. C. W. G. Guest, *Deputy Ch.*

iii. Members

1955–56 (35)	vi	Elections [Possible disqualification of a Member because of office held]. Sel. Cttee. C. Williams, *Ch.* Rep., proc., mins. of ev., apps.
(50–I)	vi	—— 2nd Rep., proc., mins. of ev., apps.
1955–56 (117)	vi	Elections [Possible disqualification of a Member because of office held]. Sel. Cttee. W. E. Elliot, *Ch* Rep., proc., mins. of ev., apps.
(145–I)	vi	—— 2nd Rep., proc., mins. of ev., app.

2. Parliament—*continued*

1955–56 Cmd.9698	xxxii	Disqualification of certain members of the Senate and House of Commons of Northern Ireland.
1955–56 (349)	ix	House of Commons Disqualification Bill. Sel. Cttee. P. Spens, *Ch.* Special Rep., proc., mins. of ev., apps.
1954–55 (11)	x	P. A. D. Baker. Certified copies of the indictment, conviction and sentence of the Court, etc.
1955–56 (32)	xxxii	Thomas J. Mitchell. Certificate of conviction and sentence of the Assize Court at Belfast on 30/11/54.
1954–55 (105)	viii	House of Commons Members' Fund. Pensions for Members. Rep.
1960–61 (75)	xvii	House of Commons Members' Fund. Government Actuary. Rep.

iv. Privileges

1956–57 (27)	vii	Complaint by Mr. Arthur Lewis, Member for West Ham, North. Cttee. R. A. Butler, *Ch.* 1st Rep., proc., mins. of ev.
(38)	vii	Complaint of a passage in the *Sunday Express* newspaper of the 16th December, 1956. Cttee. R. A. Butler, *Ch.* 2nd Rep., proc., mins. of ev.
(39)	vii	Complaint of a drawing and text in the *Evening News* newspaper. Cttee. R. A. Butler, *Ch.* 3rd Rep., mins. of ev.
(74)	vii	Complaints of a broadcast by the B.B.C., and of statements reported in the *Romford Recorder* newspaper. Cttee. R. A. Butler, *Ch.* 4th Rep., proc.
(305)	vii	Complaint by Mr. Strauss of certain actions of the London Electricity Board. Cttee. R. A. Butler, *Ch.* 5th Rep., proc., mins. of ev.
1957–58 (227)	vi	Complaint by Mr. Strauss of certain actions of the London Electricity Board. Cttee. R. A. Butler, *Ch.* Rep., proc.
1957–58 Cmnd.431	xxiv	Order in Council, May 7th, 1958, directing that the Rep. of the Judicial Cttee. on a question of law concerning the Parliamentary Privilege Act, 1770, be communicated to the House of Commons with reasons for such Rep. as delivered by their Lordships. [Whether the issue of a writ against a Member in respect of proceedings or speech by him should be treated as a breach of privilege.].
1959–60 (284–I)	vii	Complaint of a letter to a Member by Mr. Colin Jordan. Cttee. R. A. Butler, *Ch.* Rep., proc., mins. of ev.
1963–64 (247)	vi	Complaint concerning speech by the Rt. Hon. Quintin Hogg. Cttee. J. S. B. Lloyd, *Ch.* Rep., proc., mins. of ev.

2. Parliament—*continued*

v. Procedure, Statutory Instruments

1956–57 (110)	vii	Procedure. Sel. Cttee. W. E. Elliot, *Ch.* 1st Rep., proc., mins. of ev.
(211)	vii	—— 2nd Rep., proc., mins. of ev.
1957–58 (262)	vi	Procedure. Public business of the House. Sel. Cttee. J. Stuart, *Ch.* Special Rep., proc. (Formal only).
1958–59 (92–I)	vi	Procedure. Public business of the House. Sel. Cttee. J. Stuart, *Ch.* Rep., proc., mins. of ev., apps.
1961–62 (236)	vii	Procedure. Effect of Standing Order 58(2) on minorities.
1962–63 (156)	vi	Procedure. Rule relating to reference in the House of Commons to matters considered as sub judice. Sel. Cttee. I. N. Macleod, *Ch.* 1st Rep., proc., mins. of ev., apps. Sel. Cttee. I. N. Macleod, *Ch.* Rep., proc., mins. of ev., app.
(190)	vi	—— 2nd Rep., etc. Expediting the Finance Bill.
(271)	vi	—— 3rd Rep., proc.
1963–64 (248)	vi	Procedure. Form of the defence estimates. Sel. Cttee. J. S. B. Lloyd, *Ch.* 1st Rep., proc., mins. of ev., apps.
(295)	vi	—— 2nd Rep., etc. Disclosure of matters contained in the Reports of Select Committees.
(306)	vi	—— 3rd Rep.
1958–59 (262)	vii	Promotion of Private Bills. Jt. Cttee. Ld. Reading, *Ch.* Rep., proc., mins. of ev., apps.
1959–60 (222)	vii	Public petitions. Sel. Cttee. Special Rep.
1958–59 (5–III–I)	vii	Statutory Instruments. Sel. Cttee. E. G. M. Fletcher, *Ch.* Rep., proc., mins. of ev.
1963–64 (10–IX–I)	vii	Statutory Instruments. Sel. Cttee. E. G. M. Fletcher, *Ch.* 2nd Rep., proc., mins. of ev.
1961–62 Cmnd.1610	xxxi	Draft of the Statutory Orders (Special Procedure) Order, 1962.
1962–63 Cmnd.1865	xxxi	Draft of the Statutory Orders (Special Procedure) (Substitution) Order, 1962.

vi. Publications and Debates

1955–56 (288)	vi	Broadcasting (Anticipation of debates). Sel. Cttee. L. F. Heald, *Ch.* Rep., proc., mins. of ev., app.
1954–55 (91)	iii	Publications and debates reports. Sel. Cttee. S. Storey, *Ch.* Rep., proc.
(126)	iii	—— 2nd Rep., proc.
1955–56 (420)	ix	Publications and debates reports. Sel. Cttee. J. F. E. Crowder, *Ch.* Rep., proc., mins. of ev., app.
1963–64 (37)	vi	Publications and debates reports. Sel. Cttee. Rep., app.

vii. House of Lords

1955–56 (HL. 7, 66–I, 67)	iv	Powers of the House in relation to attendances of its members. Sel. Cttee. Ld. Swinton, *Ch.* Rep., proc., mins. of ev.

2. Parliament—*continued*

1956–57 (HL.16)	iv	Procedure of the House. Sel. Cttee. 1st Rep.
(HL.99)	iv	—— 2nd Rep.
1958–59 (HL.36)	v	Procedure of the House. Sel. Cttee. 1st Rep.
(HL.172)	v	—— 2nd Rep.
1959–60 (HL.79)	iv	Procedure of the House. Sel. Cttee. 1st Rep.
(HL.100)	iv	—— 2nd Rep.
1960–61 (HL.129)	iv	Procedure of the House. Sel. Cttee. 1st Rep.
1961–62 (HL.117)	v	Procedure of the House. Sel. Cttee. 1st Rep.
1962–63 (HL.123)	v	Procedure of the House. Sel. Cttee. 1st Rep.
1963–64 (HL.20A)	v	Procedure of the House. Sel. Cttee. 1st Rep.
(HL.84)	v	—— 2nd Rep.
(HL.137)	v	—— 3rd Rep.
(HL.188)	v	—— 4th Rep.
1963–64 (HL.11)	v	Privileges. Cttee. 1st Rep.
(HL.33)	v	—— 2nd Rep.
1961–62 (262)	vii	House of Lords reform. Jt. Sel. Cttee. Rep. (Formal only.).
1962–63 (38)	vi	House of Lords reform. Jt. Sel. Cttee. Ld. Kilmuir, *Ch.* Rep., proc., apps.

3. Ministers

1956–57 Cmnd.283	xv	Interception of communications [Executive power of the Secretary of State]. Cttee. of Privy Councillors. W. N. Birkett, *Ch.* Rep.
1962–63 Cmnd.2152	xxiv	Lord Denning's Report. [Profumo affair.].

4. Departments

i. Decentralisation and Devolution

1955–56 Cmd.9732	x	Provincial and local organisation and procedures of the Ministry of Agriculture, Fisheries & Food. Cttee. A. Wilson, *Ch.* Rep.
1956–57 Cmnd.53	xxvi	Council for Wales & Monmouthshire. H. T. Edwards, *Ch.* 3rd Memo. on its activities. (See Breviate III, pp. 87, 124).
1957–58 Cmnd.334	xxiv	Government administration in Wales. Text of letter addressed by the Prime Minister to the Chairman of the Council for Wales & Monmouthshire.
1958–59 Cmnd.631	xxv	Council for Wales & Monmouthshire. H. T. Edwards, *Ch.* 4th Memo. Government administration in Wales.
1957–58 Cmnd.445	xxiv	Local government and central departments in Scotland.

ii. Separate Departments

1956 Non-Parl.		Social and economic research. Inter-Dept. Cttee. G. North, *Ch.* Rep. Ld. President's Office.
1955–56 Cmd.9734	xxvii	Department of Scientific & Industrial Research. Cttee. H. Jephcott, *Ch.* Rep.

4. Departments—*continued*

1961	Non-Parl.	Management and control of research and development. Cttee. S. Zuckerman, *Ch.* Rep., apps. Office of the Minister for Science.
1963–64	Cmnd.2171 ix	Organisation of civil science. Cttee. B. St. J. Trend, *Ch.* Rep.
1955–56	Cmd.9755 xxvii	Public Trustee Office. Cttee. M. G. Holmes, *Ch.* Rep.
1955–56	Cmd.9879 xxxvi	Staffing and organisation of the Factory Inspectorate.
1958–59	Cmnd.736 xxv	Duties, organisation and staffing of the medical branch of the Factory Inspectorate.
1956–57	Cmnd.225 xxvi	Overseas information services.
1958–59	Cmnd.685 xxv	Overseas information services.
1954	Non-Parl.	Reorganisation of the Colonial Service. Colonial Office.
1955–56	Cmd.9768 xxxv	Her Majesty's Oversea Civil Service. Statement of policy regarding organisation.
1959–60	Cmnd.1193 xxvii	Service with overseas governments.
1961–62	Cmnd.1740 xxxi	Recruitment for service overseas. Future policy.
1963–64	Cmnd.2276 xi	Representational services overseas. Cttee. Ld. Plowden, *Ch.* Rep.
1957–58	Cmnd.476 xxi	Central organisation for defence.
1962–63	Cmnd.2097 xxvii	Central organisation for defence.

Note: For Defence White Papers *see* Annex 2, p. 93.

1961–62	Cmnd.1698 xxiv	Technical Co-operation. Progress Rep. by the new department.
1963–64	Cmnd.2233 xxvi	Reorganisation of the Ministry of Public Building & Works.
1963–64	Cmnd.2428 xvi	Pricing of Ministry of Aviation contracts. Inquiry. J. G. Lang, *Ch.* 1st Rep.
1964–65	Cmnd.2581 xix	—— 2nd Rep.
1963	Non-Parl.	Accommodation needs of the Scottish Record Office, Registrar-General's Office and Lyon Office. Cttee. Ld. Keith, *Ch.* Rep., apps. Scottish Home & Health Dept.

iii. Nationalised Industries

These entries list those reports of the select committees on nationalised industries which deal mainly with their control by and accountability to Parliament and links with the House. For a full list of the committees' reports, including those dealing with particular industries, see Sections V.8.ii, VI and VII.

1954–55	(121) iii	Nationalised industries. Sel. Cttee. P. Spens, *Ch.* Proc.
1955–56	(120) ix	Nationalised industries. Sel. Cttee. P. Spens, *Ch.* Special Rep., proc., mins. of ev., apps.
1956–57	(304) vii	Nationalised industries (Reports and Accounts). Sel. Cttee. P. Spens, *Ch.* Rep., proc., mins. of ev., apps.

4. Departments—*continued*

1958–59 (276)	vii	Nationalised industries (Reports and Accounts). Sel. Cttee. T. A. R. W. Low, *Ch.* Special Rep., mins. of ev., app.
1960–61 Cmnd.1337	xxvii	Financial and economic obligations of the nationalised industries. White Paper.
1961–62 (116)	vii	˙Nationalised industries. Reports of former Select Committees on nationalised industries: outcome of recommendations and conclusions. Sel. Cttee. G. R. H. Nugent, *Ch.* Rep., proc., mins. of ev., apps.

iv. Administrative Tribunals

1956–57 Cmnd.218	viii	Administrative tribunals and inquiries. Cttee. O.S. Franks, *Ch.* Rep.
1956	Non-Parl.	—— Mins. of ev., 1st–21st days.
1957	Non-Parl.	—— Mins. of ev., 22nd–27th days.
1956	Non-Parl.	—— Memoranda, Vols. I–VI.
1957	Non-Parl.	—— Apps. I, II.
1957	Non-Parl.	—— Index to evidence, apps. and memoranda.
1960	Non-Parl.	Council on Tribunals. Ld. Reading, *Ch.* 1st Rep. Ld. Chancellor's Dept. (See succeeding Ann. Reps.).
1958	Non-Parl.	Procedure in connection with statutory inquiries. Memo. Dept. of Health, Scot.
1961–62 Cmnd.1787	xxiv	Position of 'third parties' at planning appeal inquiries. Council on Tribunals. Ld. Tenby, *Ch.* Rep.
1963–64 Cmnd.2471	x	Award of costs at statutory inquiries. Council on Tribunals. Ld. Tenby & D. B. Bogle, *Ch.* Rep.

5. Civil and Colonial Service

i. Civil Service

1954–55 Cmd.9380	xii	Equal pay for men and women civil servants. Treasury Minute. (See Breviate III, pp. 263–5).
1955–56 Cmd.9613	xi	Civil Service. R. Com. R. E. Priestley, *Ch.* Rep. (see Breviate III, p. 38).
1954	Non-Parl.	—— Introductory factual memo. submitted by H. M. Treasury.
1954	Non-Parl.	—— —— Supplement. Medical and legal staffs.
1954	Non-Parl.	—— Mins. of ev., 1st–24th days.
1955	Non-Parl.	—— Mins. of ev., 25th–28th days.
1956	Non-Parl.	—— Index to mins. of ev.
1954	Non-Parl.	—— App. I. 1st Selection of supplementary statements.
1955	Non-Parl.	—— App. II. 2nd Selection of supplementary statements.
1956–57 Cmnd.232	xxv	Recruitment to the administrative class of the home civil service and the senior branch of the foreign service. Government statement and Rep. of Civil Service Com.
1958	Non-Parl.	Staff relations in the civil service. 3rd ed. [App. XII: Civil Service Pay Research Unit]. Treasury.

5. Civil and Colonial Service—*continued*

1958	Non-Parl.		Civil Service Pay Research Unit. 1st Ann. Rep. The Unit. (See succeeding Ann. Reps.).
1958–59	Cmnd.583	ix	Misuse of official facilities for the circulation of documents. Enquiry. Norman C. Brook. Rep.
1955–56	Cmd.9577	xli	Disappearance of two former Foreign Office officials [Donald Maclean and Guy Burgess]. Rep. (See Breviate III, p. 38).
1955–56	Cmd.9715	xxxvi	Security. Conference of Privy Councillors. Statement on the findings. (See Breviate III, p. 37).
1961–62	Cmnd.1681	xxiii	Security procedures in the public service. Cttee. Ld. Radcliffe, *Ch.* Rep.
1962–63	Cmnd.1871	xxiv	Vassall case. Cttee. C. C. Cunningham, *Ch.* Interim Rep.
1962–63	Cmnd.2009	xxiv	Vassall case and related matters. Tribunal. Ld. Radcliffe, *Ch.* Rep.
	Cmnd.2037	xxiv	—— Mins. of ev.
1962–63	Cmnd.2152	xxiv	Lord Denning's Report [Profumo affair].
ii. Colonial Service			*See* Annex 1, Relations with Commonwealth Countries, p. 91.

6. Local Government

i. General

1955–56	Cmd.9607	xxxvi	Messages to local authorities in England and Wales and in Scotland [Government's request for review of capital expenditure.].
1955–56	Cmd.9831	xxxvi	Local government. Areas and status of local authorities in England and Wales. White Paper.
1956–57	Cmnd.161	xxvi	Functions of county councils and county district councils in England and Wales. White Paper.
1961–1966			Local Government Com. for England. H. D. Hancock, *Ch.* Min. of Housing & Local Govt.
1961	Non-Parl.		—— Rep. no. 1. West Midlands special review area. Maps A–D and 1–11.
1962	Non-Parl.		—— —— Objections to the proposals . . . for a pattern of county boroughs for the Black Country. Inquiry. Rep.
1961	Non-Parl.		—— Rep. no. 2. West Midlands general review area. Maps A–C and 1–3.
1961	Non-Parl.		—— Rep. no. 3. East Midlands general review area. Maps A–F and 1–4.
1963	Non-Parl.		—— —— Objections to the proposal to amalgamate Leicestershire and Rutland . . . Inquiry. Rep.
1963	Non-Parl.		—— —— Objections to the proposals that . . . Huntingdonshire and the Soke of Peterborough should . . . form a new administrative county . . . and the administrative counties of Cambridgeshire and the Isle of Ely . . . should be amalgamated . . . Inquiry. Rep.
1963	Non-Parl.		—— Rep. no. 4. South Western general review area. Maps A–F and 1–7.

6. Local Government—*continued*

1965	Non-Parl.	—— —— Objections to the proposals for the area. Inquiry. Rep.
1963	Non-Parl.	—— Rep. no. 5. Tyneside special review area. Maps A–D and 1–4.
1965	Non-Parl.	—— —— Objections to the proposals for the area. Inquiry. Rep.
1963	Non-Parl.	—— Rep. no. 6. North Eastern general review area. Maps A–F and 1–4.
1965	Non-Parl.	—— —— Objections to the recommendation . . . for the constitution of a Tees-side county borough. Inquiry. Rep.
1964	Non-Parl.	—— Rep. no. 7. West Yorkshire special review area. Maps A–C and 1–12.
1964	Non-Parl.	—— Rep. no. 8. York and North Midlands general review area. Maps A–H and 1–8.
1965	Non-Parl.	—— —— Objections to the proposals . . . for the city of Nottingham and the surrounding areas. Inquiry. Rep.
1966	Non-Parl.	—— —— Objections to the proposals . . . for the city of Sheffield and the surrounding areas. Inquiry. Rep.
1966	Non-Parl.	—— —— Objections to the proposals . . . for the city of York and the surrounding area. Inquiry. Rep.
1965	Non-Parl.	—— Rep. no. 9. Lincolnshire and East Anglia general review area. Maps A–F and 1–5.
1963	Non-Parl.	Wales. Local Government Com. for Wales. G. Myrddin-Evans, *Ch.* Rep. and proposals. Maps 1–36.
1957–58 Cmnd.445 xxiv		Local government and central departments in Scotland.
1962–63 Cmnd.2067 xxxi		Modernisation of local government in Scotland.
1964	Non-Parl.	Reorganisation of local government in Scotland. Working Party. 1st Rep.

ii. Finance

1956–57 Cmnd.209 xxvi		Local government finance (England and Wales).
1958–59 (15) xvi		Local government finance (England and Wales). General Grant Order 1958. Rep. by the Minister of Housing & Local Govt. (See succeeding ann. Reps. on General Grant Orders or General Grant (Increase) Orders).
(15–1) xvi		—— Supplement.
1962	Non-Parl.	Working of the rate-deficiency grants in England and Wales. Working Party. F. L. Edwards, *Ch.* Rep., app. Min. of Housing & Local Govt.
1962–63 Cmnd.2162 xxxi		Local authority borrowing.
1955–56 Cmd.9718 xxxvi		Distribution of rateable values between different classes of property in England and Wales.
1959	Non-Parl.	Rating of plant and machinery. Cttee. E. H. Ritson, *Ch.* Rep., apps. Min. of Housing & Local Govt.

6. Local Government—*continued*

1961–62 Cmnd.1663 xxxi		Revaluation for rates in 1963 (England & Wales). The rate liability of the householder.
1962–63 Cmnd.1982 xxxi		Distribution of rateable values between different classes of property in England and Wales.
1955 Non-Parl.		Operation of the Exchequer equalisation grants in Scotland. Cttee. J. N. Browne, *Ch.* 2nd investigation. Rep. Scottish Home Dept. (See Breviate III, p. 52).
1955–56 (109)	xxii	Equalisation grant in Scotland. 2nd investigation. Rep. (See Breviate III, p. 52).
1962–63 (2)	xx	—— 3rd investigation. Rep.
1955–56 Cmd.9606	xxxvi	Valuation and rating in Scotland. (See Breviate III, p. 52).
1955 Non-Parl.		Valuation for rating of gasworks in Scotland. Working Party. A. J. Aglen, *Ch.* Rep., apps. Scottish Home Dept.
1955 Non-Parl.		Valuation for rating of waterworks in Scotland. Working Party. A. J. Aglen, *Ch.* Rep., apps. Scottish Home Dept.
1956–57 Cmnd.208	xxvi	Local government finance in Scotland.
1958–59 (16)	xvi	Local government finance (Scotland). General Grant (Scotland) Order 1958. Rep. by the Sec. of State. (See succeeding ann. Reps. on General Grant (Scotland) Orders or General Grant (Increase) (Scotland) Orders).

7. London

i. Government

1959–60 Cmnd.1164 xviii		Local government in Greater London. R. Com. E. S. Herbert, *Ch.* Rep.
1959 Non-Parl.		—— Mins. of ev., 1st–46th days.
1960 Non-Parl.		—— Mins. of ev., 47th–70th days.
1960 Non-Parl.		—— Apps. I, II.
1960 Non-Parl.		—— Index to mins. of ev.
1959 Non-Parl.		—— Memoranda of ev. from Government Departments.
1962 Non-Parl.		—— Written ev. Vols. I–V.
1961–62 Cmnd.1562 xxxi		London government. Government proposals for re-organisation.
1962 Non-Parl.		London government. The London boroughs. Rep. Min. of Housing & Local Govt.

ii. Particular Problems

1955 Non-Parl.		London transport. Cttee. S. P. Chambers, *Ch.* Rep., apps. Min. of Transport & Civil Aviation.
1956 Non-Parl.		30 m.p.h. speed limit in the London traffic area. Adv. Cttee. A. Samuels, *Ch.* Rep., apps. Min. of Transport & Civil Aviation.

7. London—*continued*

1956	Non-Parl.		Parking survey of inner London. Cttee. A. Samuels, *Ch.* Interim Rep., apps. Min. of Transport & Civil Aviation.
1958	Non-Parl.		—— Final Rep., apps.
1958	Non-Parl.		"Crush hour" travel in Central London. Cttee. for the staggering of working hours. J. Fitzgerald, *Ch.* Rep., apps. Min. of Transport & Civil Aviation.
1958–59	Cmnd.812	xix	London roads. Cttee. G. R. H. Nugent, *Ch.* Rep.
1959–60	(144)	xx	Results of the experimental introduction of a 40 m.p.h. speed limit in the London traffic area. Dept. Road Safety Cttee. J. A. Hay, *Ch.* Rep.
1959	Non-Parl.		Victoria line. London Travel Cttee. A. Samuels, *Ch.* Rep., apps. Min. of Transport & Civil Aviation.
1963	Non-Parl.		Parking—the next stage. A new look at London's parking problems.
1963–64	(226)	xix	London Transport Board. [1st] Ann. Rep. and Accounts. (See succeeding Ann. Reps.).
1957	Non-Parl.		London airport development. Cttee. P. E. Millbourn, *Ch.* Rep., apps. Min. of Transport & Civil Aviation.
1961	Non-Parl.		Planning of helicopter stations in the London area. Cttee. G. I. Morris, *Ch.* Rep., apps. Min. of Aviation.
1964	Non-Parl.		Third London airport. Inter-Dept. Cttee. G. V. Hole, *Ch.* Rep., Min. of Aviation.
1959–60	Cmnd.956	xxvii	Technical possibilities of a Thames flood barrier.
1961	Non-Parl.		Pollution of the tidal Thames. Dept. Cttee. A. J. S. Pippard, *Ch.* Rep., apps. Min. of Housing & Local Govt.
1954–55	Cmd.9467	vii	A new Queen's Hall. Cttee. L. C. Robbins, *Ch.* Rep., apps. (See Breviate III, p. 58).
1955	Non-Parl.		Litter in the Royal Parks. Cttee. J. C. Rodgers, *Ch.* Rep., apps. Min. of Works.
1955–56	(289)	ix	Underground Works (London) Bill. Sel. Cttee. T. L. Dugdale, *Ch.* Special Rep., proc., mins. of ev.
1957–58	(118–I)	vi	Park Lane Improvement Bill. Sel. Cttee. P. G. Agnew, *Ch.* Special Rep., proc., mins.•of speeches delivered by Counsel.
1957–58	Cmnd.457	x	Preservation of Downing Street. Cttee. Ld. Crawford and Balcarres, *Ch.* Rep.
1957	Non-Parl.		Future of the Regent's Park terraces. Crown Estate Com. A. M. T. Eve, *Ch.* Statement. (See Breviate III, p. 57).
1959	Non-Parl.		—— 2nd Statement.
1962	Non-Parl.		—— 3rd Statement.
1961	Non-Parl.		Future of Carlton House terrace. Crown Estate Com. A. M. T. Eve, *Ch.* Statement.

7. London—*continued*

1960–16 (HL.102) | iv | Covent Garden Market Bill. Sel. Cttee. HL. Ld. Broughshane, *Ch.* Rep., proc., mins. of ev.

1960–61 (140) iv — Covent Garden Market Bill. Sel. Cttee. A. R. Wise, *Ch.* Proc., mins. of ev.

1963 Non-Parl. — Covent Garden Market Authority. 1st Rep. & Accounts. Min. of Agric., Fish. & Food. (See succeeding Ann. Reps.).

Forestry. Adv. Cttee. W. L. Taylor, *Ch.* Min. of Works. 1963: Min. of Public Building & Works. (See Breviate III, p. 111).

1957 Non-Parl. —— 3rd Rep., apps. [Trees in Royal Parks].
1960 Non-Parl. —— 4th Rep. Trees in Kensington Gardens.
1962 Non-Parl. —— 5th Rep. Trees in Richmond Park.
1963 Non-Parl. —— 6th Rep. Trees in Hampton Court and Bushy Parks.
1964 Non-Parl. —— 7th Rep. Trees in Greenwich Park.

1962–63 Cmnd.1952 xxxi — London: employment, housing, land.

1964 Non-Parl. — Offices. Statement by H.M. Government [to encourage the building of offices outside London]. Prime Minister's Office.

II. NATIONAL FINANCE

To show the relationship of some of the papers below to others dealing with economic policy, these have been brought together, with a selection of other relevant papers, to show the efforts to control the economy as a whole, in Section V, p. 43.

1955–56 Cmd.9474 xxvii — Taxation of profits and income. R.Com. Ld. Radcliffe, *Ch.* Final Rep., apps., index. (See Breviate III, pp. 68–71).
1952 Non-Parl. —— Mins. of ev., 1st–17th days.
1954 Non-Parl. —— Mins. of ev., 18th–21st days.
1955 Non-Parl. —— Index to mins. of ev.

1956–57 Cmnd.6 xxvi — Customs duties (dumping and subsidies). Memo. explaining the ways and means resolution.

1957–58 (250) x — Customs Duties (Dumping and Subsidies) Act, 1957. [1st] Ann. Rep. (See succeeding Ann. Reps.).

1957–58 Cmnd.304 xxiv — Import duties. Memo. explaining the ways and means resolution.

1959–60 (336) xii — Import Duties Act, 1958. [1st] Ann. Rep. (See succeeding Ann. Reps.).

1956–57 Cmnd.132 xxvi — Capital investment in the coal, gas and electricity industries. (See annual Papers in next three sessions. Information subsequently in Public investment in Great Britain, see next entry.).

1960–61 Cmnd.1203 xxvii — Public investment in Great Britain. (See annual Papers in next three sessions).

1960–61 Cmnd.1338 xxvii — Government expenditure below the line [repayable loans to nationalised industries, other public bodies, private industry and for overseas assistance]. (See annual Papers in next three sessions).

1961–62 Cmnd.1710 xxxi	Taxation of short-term gains.
1963–64 Cmnd.2300 xix	Turnover taxation. Cttee. G. W. H. Richardson, *Ch.* Rep.
1963–64 Cmnd.2347 xxvi	Scheme for an accounts basis for income tax on company profits.
1960–61 Cmnd.1432 xx	Control of public expenditure. Cttee. Ld. Plowden, *Ch.* Rep.
1962–63 Cmnd.2162 xxxi	Local authority borrowing.
1963–64 Cmnd.2235 xxi	Public expenditure in 1963–64 and 1967–68.
1962–63 Cmnd.2014 xxxi	Reform of the Exchequer accounts.
1960–61 Cmnd.1345 xxvii	Financial agreement with the Isle of Man.

III. BANKING AND FINANCIAL INSTITUTIONS

To facilitate a general view of the papers relating to the control of the economy as a whole, some of those listed below have been brought together with other relevant Papers on economic policy and set out in Section V, pp. 41–44. In the *Breviate of Parliamentary Papers, 1940–1954*, many papers on this topic were concerned with monetary policy and were listed in Section III, but in this period policies on these matters emphasised trade with Europe, industrial growth, productivity, regional economic development, etc., and the papers are more conveniently presented as a group in Section V.

1956–57 Cmnd.3 ix	Cheque endorsement. Cttee. A. A. Mocatta, *Ch.* Rep.
1957–58 Cmnd.350 viii	Allegations of improper disclosure of information relating to the raising of the Bank Rate. Tribunal. H. L. Parker, *Ch.* Rep.
1958 Non-Parl.	—— Proc., mins. of ev. Home Office.
1958–59 Cmnd.827 xvii	Working of the monetary system. Cttee. Ld. Radcliffe, *Ch.* Rep.
1960 Non-Parl.	—— Mins. of ev., 1st–59th days. Treasury.
1960 Non-Parl.	—— Memoranda of ev. Vols. 1–3.
1961–62 Cmnd.1656 xxxvii	Arrangements for borrowing by the International Monetary Fund.
1962–63 Cmnd.2145 xi	Decimal currency. Cttee. Ld. Halsbury, *Ch.* Rep.
1959–60 Cmnd.915 xxvii	Powers of investment of trustees in Great Britain [powers to invest in wide range of fixed interest securities and in shares of certain companies].

IV. AGRICULTURE AND FOOD SUPPLY

1. General: Production, Supply, Output

1955–56 Cmd.9732 x	Provincial and local organisation and procedures of the Ministry of Agriculture, Fisheries and Food. Cttee. A. Wilson, *Ch.* Rep.
1956–57 Cmnd.23 xxvi	Long-term assurances for agriculture.
	Agricultural Improvement Council for England and Wales. Min. of Agric., Fish. & Food. (See Breviate III, p. 76.)

1. General: Production, Supply, Output—*continued*

1957	Non-Parl.		—— 3rd Rep., 1950–56. E. A. Hitchman, *Ch.*
1960	Non-Parl.		—— 4th Rep., 1956–59. E. A. Hitchman, *Ch.*
1963	Non-Parl.		—— 4th and Final Rep., 1959–62. A. J. D. Winnifrith, *Ch.*

1958–59 Cmnd.553   xxv   Assistance for small farmers.

1960–61 Cmnd.1249 xxvii   Agriculture. Rep. on talks between the Agricultural Departments and the Farmers' Unions.

1961   Non-Parl.   Scale of enterprise in farming. Natural Resources (Technical) Cttee. Sub-Cttee. S. Zuckerman, *Ch.* Rep., apps. Office of the Minister for Science.

1958–59 Cmnd.547   viii   Grassland utilisation. Cttee. S. Caine, *Ch.* Rep.

1955–56 Cmd.9631   x   Mid-Wales investigation. Welsh Agricultural Land Sub-Com. J. C. Wynne Finch, *Ch.* Rep.

1955–56 Cmd.9809   xxxvi   Mid-Wales investigation report. Conclusions on recommendations.

1956   Non-Parl.   Monmouthshire moors investigation. Welsh Agricultural Land Sub-Com. J. C. Wynne Finch, *Ch.* Rep. (App. A consists of Rep. on Drainage and sea defences, by C. H. Dobbie). Min. of Agric., Fish. & Food.

1958   Non-Parl.   Technical problems of Welsh agriculture. Agricultural Improvement Council for England and Wales. Cttee. F. L. Engledow, *Ch.* Rep., apps. Min. of Agric., Fish. & Food.

1955–56 Cmd.9759   x   Hill lands (North of Scotland). Com. Ld. Balfour of Burleigh, *Ch.* Rep.

1958–59 Cmnd.785   xxv   Review of highland policy.

1961   Non-Parl.   Making an upland farm pay. The Glenlivet experiment. Rep., app. Dept. of Agric. & Fish., Scot.

1964   Non-Parl.   Land use in the Highlands and Islands. Adv. Panel. Ld. Cameron (J. Cameron), *Ch.* Rep., app. Dept. of Agric. & Fish., Scot.

Toxic chemicals in agriculture. Working Party. S. Zuckerman, *Ch.* (See Breviate III, pp. 87–8.)

1955   Non-Parl.   —— Rep., apps. Risks to wild life. Min. of Agric., Fish. & Food.

1961   Non-Parl.   Toxic chemicals in agriculture and food storage. Research Study Group. H. G. Sanders, *Ch.* Rep., apps. Min. of Agric., Fish. & Food.

1964   Toxic chemicals [pesticides]. Agricultural Research Council. Cttee. A. C. Frazer, *Ch.* Rep., apps. (not published by H.M.S.O.).

1964   Non-Parl.   Persistent organochlorine pesticides. Adv. Cttee. J. W. Cook, *Ch.* Rep., apps. and Supplementary Rep. Min. of Agric., Fish. & Food.

2. Production and Marketing of Particular Products

1955–56 Cmd.9519	xxxvi	Future arrangements for the marketing of sugar. (See Breviate III, p. 94).
1957–58 (306)	xvii	Sugar Board. [1st] Rep. and Accounts (see succeeding Ann. Reps.).
1955–56 Cmd.9805	x	Proposed British egg marketing scheme. Inquiry. G. G. Baker. Rep.
1956	Non-Parl.	British egg marketing scheme, 1956. Min. of Agric., Fish. & Food.
1956–57 Cmnd.154	xii	Export of live cattle to the continent for slaughter. Cttee. Ld. Balfour of Burleigh, *Ch.* Rep.
1959–60 Cmnd.1140	viii	Proposed experimental importation of charollais cattle. Cttee. Ld. Terrington, *Ch.* Rep.
1963	Non-Parl.	British livestock breeding. The way ahead. Nat. Livestock Breeding Conference. Summary of procs. Min. of Agric., Fish. & Food.
1963–64 Cmnd.2282	xvi	Fatstock and carcase meat marketing and distribution. Cttee. W. R. Verdon-Smith, *Ch.* Rep.
1956	Non-Parl.	Scottish milk marketing scheme, 1933 (incorporating amendments . . . up to and including the 1st May, 1956). Dept. of Agric., Scot.
1959–60 Cmnd.1147	xix	Milk composition in the United Kingdom. Inter-Dept. Cttee. J. W. Cook, *Ch.* Rep.

Economics of milk production. National Investigation. Reps. Min. of Agric., Fish. & Food.

1960	Non-Parl.	—— Costs and efficiency in milk production, 1955–1957. D. H. Dinsdale, *Ch.*
1963	Non-Parl.	—— Aspects of dairy economics, 1957–1960.
1964	Non-Parl.	—— Costs and efficiency in milk production, 1960–1962. L. Napolitan, *Ch.*

1961–62 Cmnd.1597	xviii	Remuneration of milk distributors in the United Kingdom. Cttee. G. F. Thorold, *Ch.* Rep.
1963	Non-Parl.	Milk marketing scheme, 1933 (as amended). Complaint by Quality Milk Producers Ltd. Cttee. D. Karmel, *Ch.* Rep., apps. Min. of Agric., Fish. & Food.
1961	Non-Parl.	Model dairy byelaws. Cttee. J. A. B. Smith, *Ch.* Rep., apps. Dept. of Health, Scot.
1955–56 Cmd.9588	xxvi	Development of pig production in the United Kingdom. Adv. Cttee. H. G. Howitt, *Ch.* Rep.
1955–56 Cmd.9795	xxvi	Pigs and bacon. Reorganisation Com. C.I.S. Bosanquet, *Ch.* Rep.
1956–57 Cmnd.24	xxvi	Policy for the development of the pig industry in the United Kingdom.
1958–59 Cmnd.821	xxv	Transfer free of charge of five pig progeny testing stations to the Pig Industry Development Authority. Treasury Minute.

2. Production and Marketing of Particular Products—*continued*

1958	Non-Parl.	Sheep industry in Britain. Natural Resources (Technical) Cttee. S. Zuckerman, *Ch.* Rep., apps. D.S.I.R.
1961	Non-Parl.	Sheep recording and progeny testing. Cttee. I. R. Morris, *Ch.* Rep., apps. Min. of Agric., Fish. & Food.
1958	Non-Parl.	British wool marketing scheme, 1950. Complaints made by the Country Wool Merchants Association and the Wool Federation of Scotland. Cttee. R. O'Sullivan, *Ch.* Rep., apps. Min. of Agric., Fish. & Food.
1962	Non-Parl.	British wool marketing scheme, 1950. Complaints made by the Scottish Wool Trades Consultative Cttee. Cttee. D. Karmel, *Ch.* Rep., apps. Dept. of Agric. & Fish., Scot.
1955	Non-Parl.	National stud policy and methods of operation. Cttee. P. L. Loraine, *Ch.* Rep. Min. of Agric., Fish. & Food.
1954–55	Cmd.9376 vii	Slaughterhouses (Scotland). Inter-Dept. Cttee. J. J. W. Handford, *Ch.* Rep. (See Breviate III, pp. 105–6).
1955–56	Cmd.9542 xxvii	Slaughterhouses (England & Wales). Inter-Dept. Cttee. R. Herbert, *Ch.* Rep. (See Breviate III, p. 105).
1955–56	Cmd.9761 xxxvi	Slaughterhouses. A policy to regulate the provision of slaughterhouses in England and Wales.
1956–57	Cmnd.243 xxvi	Recommended minimum standards for the construction, lay-out and equipment of slaughterhouses in England and Wales.
1956–57	Cmnd.61 xiv	Horticultural marketing. Cttee. Ld. Runciman, *Ch.* Rep.
1959–60	Cmnd.880 xxvii	Policy for the improvement of production and marketing of horticultural produce.
1961	Non-Parl.	Some problems of horticultural co-operative marketing in England and Wales. Dept. Working Party. J. Godber, Ld. Waldegrave, *Ch.* Rep., apps. Min. of Agric., Fish. & Food.
1962	Non-Parl.	Potato marketing scheme, 1955. Draft amendments. Explanatory notes. Min. of Agric., Fish. & Food.
1962	Non-Parl.	—— as amended to May 1, 1962.
1957–58	Cmnd.300 vii	Transactions in seeds. Cttee. B. C. Engholm, *Ch.* Rep.
1959–60	Cmnd.1092 viii	—— Rep. Plant breeders' rights.
1955	Non-Parl.	Myxomatosis. Adv. Cttee. Ld. St. Aldwyn, *Ch.* 2nd Rep. Min. of Agric. & Fish. (See Breviate III, p. 109).
1961–62	Cmnd.1664 viii	Fowl pest policy. Cttee. A. Plant, *Ch.* Rep.

2. Production and Marketing of Particular Products—*continued*

1962		Antibiotics in animal feeding. Agricultural Research Council & Medical Research Council. Jt. Cttee. Ld. Netherthorpe, *Ch.* Rep., apps. (not published by H.M.S.O.).
1961	Non-Parl.	Red Deer Com. 1st Ann. Rep. Dept. of Agric. & Fish., Scot. (see succeeding Ann. Reps. and Breviate III, p. 108).

3. Forestry

1956	Non-Parl.	Hedgerow and farm timber. Cttee. Ld. Merthyr, *Ch.* Rep., apps. Forestry Com.
1956	Non-Parl.	Marketing of woodland produce. Cttee. H. Watson, *Ch.* Rep., apps. [The Apps. contain extracts of evidence submitted.] Forestry Com.
1957	Non-Parl.	Forestry, agriculture and marginal land. Natural Resources (Technical) Cttee. S. Zuckerman, *Ch.* Rep., apps. D.S.I.R.
1958–59 Cmnd.686	xiii	Forest of Dean. Cttee. T. P. Creed, *Ch.* Rep.
1963–64 (280)	vii	New Forest Bill [Lords]. Sel. Cttee. E. A. Legge-Bourke, *Ch.* Proc., mins. of ev.
1963–64 (HL.88)	v	New Forest Bill [H.L.]. Sel. Cttee. HL. Ld. Broughshane, *Ch.* Rep., proc., mins. of ev.
		Forestry. Adv. Cttee. W. L. Taylor, *Ch.* Min. of Works. 1963: Min. of Public Building & Works. (See Breviate III, p. 111).
1957	Non-Parl.	—— 3rd Rep., apps. [Trees in Royal Parks.]
1960	Non-Parl.	—— 4th Rep. Trees in Kensington Gardens.
1962	Non-Parl.	—— 5th Rep. Trees in Richmond Park.
1963	Non-Parl.	—— 6th Rep. Trees in Hampton Court and Bushy Parks.
1964	Non-Parl.	—— 7th Rep. Trees in Greenwich Park.

4. Land Drainage, Coast Protection

1959–60 Cmnd.916	xxvii	Land drainage in England and Wales. (see Breviate III, pp. 114–15).
1962	Non-Parl.	Irrigation in Great Britain. Natural Resources (Technical) Cttee. Study Group F. H. Garner, *Ch.* Rep., apps. Office of the Minister for Science.
1962	Non-Parl.	Oceanographic and meteorological research in relation to sea defence. Adv. Cttee. J. Proudman, *Ch.* 1st Rep. [Floods]. Min. of Agric., Fish. & Food.

5. Common Land

1957–58 Cmnd.462	x	Common land. R.Com. W. I. Jennings, *Ch.* Rep.
1956	Non-Parl.	—— Mins. of ev., 1st–12th days.
1957	Non-Parl.	—— Mins. of ev., 13th–49th days.
1958	Non-Parl.	—— App.
1958	Non-Parl.	—— Index.

6. Fishing

1960–61 Cmnd.1266	xv	Fishing industry. Cttee. A. Fleck, *Ch.* Rep.

6. Fishing—*continued*

1960–61	Cmnd.1453 xxvii	Fishing industry.
1959	Non-Parl.	Weekly close time for salmon fishing. Investigation. Rep., apps. Scottish Home Dept.
1960–61	Cmnd.1350 xv	Salmon and freshwater fisheries. Cttee. Ld. Bledisloe, *Ch.* Rep.
1962–63	Cmnd.2096 xvii	Scottish salmon and trout fisheries. Cttee. Ld. Hunter (J. O. M. Hunter), *Ch.* 1st Rep.
1964–65	Cmnd.2691 xv	—— 2nd Rep.
1963	Non-Parl.	Grey seals and fisheries. Consultative Cttee. E. B. Worthington, *Ch.* Rep. Nature Conservancy.

V. ECONOMIC POLICY AND PLANNING; TRADE AND INDUSTRY

Certain of the papers from other sections have been inserted here to provide a broad picture of the efforts to examine and control the economy as a whole.

1. Statistical Information Relating to the Control of the Economy

While it is not possible to mention here all the statistical publications likely to be needed by someone making a detailed study of the British economy, the following list will be a useful guide to the more important general series. Several of the publications listed below began either during or soon after World War II; others were started or greatly expanded on the recommendations of the Radcliffe Committee on the Working of the Monetary System; yet others were produced to meet the needs of particular government policies, e.g., prices and incomes, regional economic planning, etc. Attention is drawn particularly to the *Economic Survey*, the *Preliminary Estimates of National Income and Expenditure* and the *U.K. Balance of Payments*. These papers, which in the years 1940–54 formed an important element in economic thought on the control of the economy, underwent various changes in presentation in the period under review.

Economic Survey. See Annuals p. 96. Replaced in 1963 by the *Economic Report*, issued as a Supplement to the March issue of *Economic Trends*.

National Income and Expenditure. Preliminary estimates. See Annuals p. 97. From session 1962–63 onwards they become *Preliminary Estimates of National Income and Balance of Payments*. See also the quarterly figures in *Economic Trends*, from January 1957, and the annual *National Income and Expenditure* 'Blue Book', first published in 1952.

U.K. Balance of Payments. See Annuals p. 97. Replaced in March, 1963, by quarterly figures in *Economic Trends*. See also the *Preliminary Estimates of National Income and Balance of Payments* from session 1962–63, and the annual publication, *U.K. Balance of Payments*, first published in 1963.

Statistics on Incomes, Prices, Employment and Production, published quarterly since 1962.

Financial Statistics, published monthly since May, 1962.

Abstract of Regional Statistics, published annually since 1965. *Digest of Scottish Statistics*, twice a year since 1953. *Digest of Welsh Statistics*, annual since 1954.

The *Annual Abstract of Statistics* and the *Monthly Digest of Statistics* both contain a great deal of information of relevance for the control of the economy, and the former contains an Index of Sources.

The monthly periodical *Economic Trends* has published many special statistical articles, including several on developments in official economic statistics, and these have been reprinted in the Studies in Official Statistics series, see p. 101.

2. Trade Policy Generally

1954–55 Cmd.9413	xviii	General Agreement on Tariffs and Trade. Statement of policy with revised text of the Agreement and related documents.
1954–55 Cmnd.9414	xviii	General Agreement on Tariffs and Trade. Documents relating to the ninth session of the contracting parties.
1955–56 Cmd.9779	xlii	Geneva tariff negotiations, 1956. Rep.
1961–62 Cmnd.1804	xxxviii	Geneva tariff negotiations, 1960–62. Rep.
1957–58 Cmnd.305	xxiv	Proposed implementation by the U.K. of the convention on nomenclature for the classification of goods in customs tariffs.

3. Economic Relations with Europe and the Commonwealth

i. Europe

1962	Non-Parl.	Treaty establishing the European Coal and Steel Community. Paris, April 18, 1951. Translation from the Official and Authentic Text. Foreign Office.
1954–55 Cmd.9346	xviii	European Coal and Steel Community. Agreement concerning relations between the U.K. . . . and the E.C.S.C.
1956–57 Cmnd.72	xxvi	European Free Trade Area. U.K. memo. to the Organisation for European Economic Co-operation.
1958–59 Cmnd.641	xxx	Negotiations for a European Free Trade Area. Documents.
1958–59 Cmnd.648	xxx	Negotiations for a European Free Trade Area. Rep.
1958–59 Cmnd.823	xxx	European Free Trade Association. Stockholm draft plan.
1959–60 Cmnd.906	xxxiv	European Free Trade Association. Text of Convention, etc.
Cmnd.906 –I	xxxiv	—— Text of schedules to Annex B to Convention, etc.
1962	Non-Parl.	Treaty establishing the European Economic Community. Rome, March 25, 1957. Translation from the Official and Authentic text. Foreign Office.
1961–62 Cmnd.1565	xxxvi	The U.K. and the European Economic Community. Text of the statement made by the Lord Privy Seal at the meeting with Ministers of member states.
1961–62 Cmnd.1805	xxxvi	The U.K. and the E.E.C. Rep. by the Lord Privy Seal on the meeting with Ministers of member states . . . Brussels, Aug., 1962.
1962–63 Cmnd.1847	xxxvi	—— Rep. . . . on the meeting . . . Oct. 25–27, 1962.
Cmnd.1910	xxxvi	—— Rep. . . . on the meeting . . . Dec. 19 and 20, 1962.
1962–63 Cmnd.1882	xxxvi	The U.K. and the European communities. Rep. by the Lord Privy Seal.

3. Economic Relations with Europe and the Commonwealth—*continued*

ii. Commonwealth and Developing Countries. See Annex 1, Relations with Commonwealth Countries, p. 91.

4. Fiscal and Monetary Policy

1956–57	Cmnd.132	xxvi	Capital investment in the coal, gas and electricity industries. (See annual Papers in next three sessions. Information subsequently in Public investment in Great Britain, see next entry).
1960–61	Cmnd.1203	xxvii	Public investment in Great Britain. (See annual Papers in next three sessions.).
1960–61	Cmnd.1338	xxvii	Government expenditure below the line. (See annual Papers in next three sessions).
1960–61	Cmnd.1432	xx	Control of public expenditure. Cttee. Ld. Plowden, *Ch.* Rep.
1963–64	Cmnd.2235	xxi	Public expenditure in 1963–64 and 1967–68.
1958–59	Cmnd.827	xvii	Working of the monetary system. Cttee. Ld. Radcliffe, *Ch.* Rep.
1960	Non-Parl.		—— Mins. of ev., 1st–59th days. Treasury.
1960	Non-Parl.		—— Memoranda of ev. Vols. 1–3.
1961–62	Cmnd.1656	xxxvii	Arrangements for borrowing by the International Monetary Fund.
1964	Non-Parl.		Economic situation. Statement. Prime Minister's Office.

5. Prices, Incomes and Wages Policy

1958	Non-Parl.		Prices, productivity and incomes. Council. Ld. Cohen, *Ch.* The Council.
1958	Non-Parl.		—— 2nd Rep.
1959	Non-Parl.		—— 3rd Rep.
1961	Non-Parl.		—— 4th Rep. Ld. Heyworth, *Ch.*
1961–62	Cmnd.1626	xxxi	Incomes policy: the next step.
1962–63	Cmnd.1844	xxxi	National Incomes Commission. (For a list of the Commission's reps. see p. 61).

6. Economic Growth

			National Economic Development Council. Reps.
1963	Non-Parl.		—— Growth of the U.K. economy to 1966.
1963	Non-Parl.		—— Conditions favourable to faster growth.
1963	Non-Parl.		—— Export trends.
1964	Non-Parl.		—— Growth of the economy.
1964	Non-Parl.		—— Construction industry.

7. Regional Development

1960–61	(291)	xv	Local Employment Act, 1960. [1st] Ann. Rep. (See succeeding Ann. Reps.).
1963–64	Cmnd.2206	xxvi	The North East. Programme for regional development and growth.
1964	Non-Parl.		South East study 1961–1981. Rep., apps., index. Min. of Housing & Local Govt.
1963–64	Cmnd.2308	xxvi	South East England.

7. Regional Development—*continued*

1962–63 Cmnd.1952 xxxi	London: employment, housing, land.
1964 Non-Parl.	Offices. Statement by H.M. Government [to encourage the building of offices outside London]. Prime Minister's Office.
1956–57 Cmnd.53 xxvi	Council for Wales & Monmouthshire. H. T. Edwards, *Ch.* 3rd Memo. on its activities: rural and industrial development.
1962–63 Cmnd.1950 xxv	Welsh holiday industry. Council for Wales & Monmouthshire. R. I. Aaron, *Ch.* Rep.
1964 Non-Parl.	Depopulation in mid-Wales. Cttee. W. M. Ogden, A. Beacham, *Ch.* Rep., apps. Min. of Housing & Local Govt.
1961–62 Cmnd.1835 xix	Economy of Northern Ireland. Jt. Working Party. R. L. Hall, *Ch.* Rep.
1962–63 Cmnd.2004 xxiv	Scottish Development Department. [1st] Ann. Rep. (See succeeding Ann. Reps.).
1963–64 Cmnd.2188 xxvi	Central Scotland. Programme for development and growth.

8. Particular Industries; Nationalised Industries

i. Particular Industries

1956–57 Cmnd.269 ix	Building legislation in Scotland. Cttee. C. W. G. Guest, *Ch.* Rep.
1962 Non-Parl.	Survey of problems before the construction industries. H. C. Emmerson. Rep., apps. Min. of Works.
1963 Non-Parl.	Winter building. Cttee. I. T. M. Davis, *Ch.* Interim Review, apps. Min. of Public Building & Works.
1963–64 Cmnd.2279 ix	Building regulations. Adv. Cttee. R. M. Wynne-Edwards, *Ch.* 1st Rep.
1963–64 (36) xxvi	Collapse of a precast concrete building. Building Research Station. Technical Statement.
1963–64 Cmnd.2228 xxvi	A national building agency.
1964 Non-Parl.	Construction industry. N.E.D.C. Rep.
1964 Non-Parl.	Building research and information services. Working Party. D.E.W. Parish, *Ch.* Rep., apps. Min. of Public Building & Works.
1964 Non-Parl.	Placing and management of contracts for building and civil engineering work. Cttee. G. H. Banwell, *Ch.* Rep., apps. Min. of Public Building & Works.
1964 Non-Parl.	Organisation and practices for building and civil engineering. Working Party. W. M. Younger, *Ch.* Rep., apps. Min. of Public Building & Works.
1958–59 Cmnd.744 xxv	Reorganisation of the cotton industry.
1964 Non-Parl.	Cutlery and silverware trades in Sheffield and district. Jt. Adv. Cttee. R. Hillier, *Ch.* Rep., apps. Min. of Labour.

8. Particular Industries; Nationalised Industries—*continued*

1963	Non-Parl.		Engineering design. Cttee. G. B. R. Feilden, *Ch.* Rep., apps. D.S.I.R.
1955–56	(53)	xxix	Postponement and remission of payments due from the National Film Finance Corporation. Bd. of Trade. Statement.
1958–59	(268)	ix	British Film Fund Agency. 1st Ann. Rep. & Accounts. (See succeeding Ann. Reps.).
1958–59	(261)	xxv	Cinematograph Film Production (Special Loans) Act, 1949. Bd. of Trade. Statement.
1961–62	(250)	xxi	—— Statement.
1963–64	Cmnd.2324	xxvi	Structure and training practices of the films industry. Cinematograph Films Council. Recommendations.
1958–59	Cmnd.663	.xv	Hallmarking. Dept. Cttee. J. L. Stone, *Ch.* Rep.
1961–62	Cmnd.1808	xx	Industrial designs. Dept. Cttee. K. R. H. Johnston, *Ch.* Rep.
1954–55	(70)	vi	Iron and Steel Holding and Realisation Agency. [1st] Rep. & Accounts. (See succeeding Ann. Reps.) (see Breviate III, p. 149).
1954–55	(138)	vi	Iron and Steel Board. [1st] Ann. Rep. (See succeeding Ann. Reps.) (see Breviate III, p. 149).
1956–57	(214)	xv	Development in the iron and steel industry. Iron and Steel Bd. A. F. Forbes, *Ch.* Special Rep.
1960–61	(164)	xviii	Development in the iron and steel industry. Iron and Steel Board. Special Rep.
1963	Non-Parl.		Research in the iron and steel industry. Iron and Steel Board. Technical Adv. Panel. A. Wilson, *Ch.* Special Rep., apps. Min. of Power.
1960	Non-Parl.		Machine tool industry. Adv. Council. Sub-Cttee. S. S. C. Mitchell, *Ch.* Rep., apps. Bd. of Trade.
1961	Non-Parl.		Shipbuilding. Adv. Cttee. Sub-Cttee. L. J. Dunnett, *Ch.* Rep. on prospects. Min. of Transport.
1961	Non-Parl.		Shipbuilding orders placed overseas by British shipowners. Rep. by Messrs. Peat, Marwick, Mitchell & Co. Min. of Transport.
1963	Non-Parl.		Production of building components in shipyards. Rep. Min. of Public Building & Works.
1961	Non-Parl.		Productivity in letterpress printing. Investigation. Working Group. Rep., apps. D.S.I.R.

ii. Nationalised Industries

The following list brings together the reports by select committees on nationalised industries, which are defined as 'those established by statute, whose controlling boards are appointed by Ministers of the Crown, and whose annual receipts are not wholly or mainly derived from moneys provided by Parliament or advanced from the Exchequer'. Initially the committee was to 'obtain information on current policy and practices not the responsibility of the Minister, nor concerned with wages, day-to-day administration, or dealt with by other formal machinery'. Several White Papers are also included. For other reports on

8. Particular Industries; Nationalised Industries—*continued*

these industries, see the relevant entries in Sections VI, Fuel and Power, and VII, Transport. The iron and steel industry, which had been nationalised, was denationalised by the Iron and Steel Act, 1953, and not re-nationalised until 1967. (See Breviate III, pp. 148–9). Reports on this industry will be found in section 8.i, above.

1954–55 (121)	iii	Nationalised industries. Sel. Cttee. P. Spens, *Ch.* Proc.
1955–56 (120)	ix	Nationalised industries. Sel. Cttee. P. Spens, *Ch.* Special Rep., proc., mins. of ev., apps.
1956–57 (304)	vii	Nationalised industries (Reports and Accounts). Sel. Cttee. P. Spens, *Ch.* Rep., proc., mins. of ev., apps.
1957–58 (187–I)	vi	Nationalised industries (Reports and Accounts) [Coal]. Sel. Cttee. T. A. R. W. Low, *Ch.* Rep., proc., mins. of ev., apps.
1958–59 Cmnd.585	xxv	Minister of Transport and Civil Aviation and the Chairman of the British Transport Com. Exchange of correspondence. [Railway deficit].
1957–58 (304)	vi	Nationalised industries (Reports and Accounts). [Air corporations]. Sel. Cttee. T. A. R. W. Low, *Ch.* Special Rep., proc. (Formal only).
1958–59 (213)	vii	—— Sel. Cttee. T. A. R. W. Low, *Ch.* Rep., proc., mins. of ev., apps.
1959–60 (339)	vii	—— Sel. Cttee. Special Rep. Replies of the Air Corporations and comments of the Minister.
1958–59 (276)	vii	Nationalised industries (Reports and Accounts). [General problem of link with the House]. Sel. Cttee. T. A. R. W. Low, *Ch.* Special Rep., mins. of ev., app.
1959–60 (254)	vii	Nationalised industries. British Railways. Sel. Cttee. T. A. R. W. Low, *Ch.* Rep.
(254–I)	vii	—— Rep., proc., mins. of ev., apps.
1960–61 (163)	vii	—— Observations of the B.T.C. and the Minister of Transport.
1960–61 Cmnd.1248	xxvii	Reorganisation of the nationalised transport undertakings. White Paper.
1960–61 Cmnd.1337	xxvii	Financial and economic obligations of the nationalised industries. White Paper.
1960–61 (280)	vii	Nationalised industries. Gas industry. Sel. Cttee. T. A. R. W. Low, *Ch.* Vol. I. Rep., proc.
(280–I)	vii	—— Vol. II. Mins. of ev., apps., index.
1961–62 (218)	vii	—— Sel. Cttee. Special Rep. Observations of the Gas Council and of the Minister of Power.
1963–64 (150)	vii	—— Sel. Cttee. 2nd Special Rep. Further observations of the Minister of Power.
1961–62 (116)	vii	Nationalised industries. Reports of former Select Committees on nationalised industries: outcome of recommendations and conclusions. Sel. Cttee. G. R. H. Nugent, *Ch.* Rep., proc., mins. of ev., apps.

8. Particular Industries; Nationalised Industries—*continued*

1961–62	(269)	vii	Nationalised industries. Electricity supply industry. Sel. Cttee. G. R. H. Nugent, *Ch.* 2nd Special Rep., proc. (Formal only.).
1962–63	(236–I)	vi	—— Sel. Cttee. G. R. H. Nugent, *Ch.* Vol. I. Rep., proc.
	(236–II)	vii	—— —— Vol. II. Mins. of ev.
	(236–III)	vii	—— —— Vol. III. Apps., index.
1963–64	(67)	vii	—— Sel. Cttee. 1st Special Rep. Observations of the Electricity Council and the Minister of Power.
1963–64	(5)	xxvi	Financial problems of B.O.A.C. White Paper.
1963–64	(240)	vii	Nationalised industries. B.O.A.C. Sel. Cttee. G. R. H. Nugent, *Ch.* Vol. I. Rep., proc.
	(240–I)	vii	—— Vol. II. Mins. of ev., apps., index.

9. Research and Development

1956	Non-Parl.	Social and economic research. Inter-Dept. Cttee. G. North, *Ch.* Rep. Ld. President's Office.
1955–56	Cmd.9734 xxvii	Department of Scientific and Industrial Research. Cttee. H. Jephcott, *Ch.* Rep.
1959	Non-Parl.	Estimates of resources devoted to scientific and engineering research and development in British manufacturing industry, 1955. Rep., apps. D.S.I.R.
1960	Non-Parl.	Industrial research and development expenditure, 1958. Council. Cttee. C. F. Carter, *Ch.* Rep., app. D.S.I.R.
1960	Non-Parl.	Research and development requirements of the ship-building and marine engineering industries. Council. Cttee. Rep. D.S.I.R.
1961	Non-Parl.	Management and control of research and development. Cttee. S. Zuckerman, *Ch.* Rep., apps. Office of the Minister for Science.
1963–64	Cmnd.2171 ix	Organisation of civil science. Cttee. B. St. J. Trend, *Ch.* Rep.
1958	Non-Parl.	Research for industry. A summary of work done by the industrial research associations in the government scheme. D.S.I.R. (Previously part of D.S.I.R.'s ann. rep. see succeeding annual publications).

10. Monopolies and Restrictive Practices

1955–1964		Monopolies and Restrictive Practices Com. 1957–58: Monopolies Com. D. A. S. Cairns, *Ch.* 1954–1956. R. F. Levy, *Ch.* 1956–1966. Reps. (See Breviate III, pp. 156–64).
1955–56	Cmd.9504 xxiv	—— Collective discrimination: exclusive dealing, collective boycotts, aggregated rebates, and other discriminatory trade practices.
1955–56	(56) xxiv	—— Certain semi-manufactures of copper and copper-based alloys.
	(133) xxiv	—— Pneumatic tyres.
	(222) xxiv	—— Sand and gravel in Central Scotland.

10. Monopolies and restricted Practices—*continued*

1955–56	(294)	xxiv	—— Hard fibre cordage.
	(328)	xxiv	—— Certain rubber footwear.
	(366)	xxiv	—— Linoleum.
1956–57	(13)	xvii	—— Certain industrial and medical gases.
	(14)	xvii	—— Standard metal windows and doors.
	(15)	xvii	—— Tea.
	(16)	xvi	—— Electronic valves and cathode ray tubes.
	(42)	xvi	—— Electrical and allied machinery and plant.
1957–58	(274)	xvi	—— Imported timber. Whether and to what extent the recommendation of the Commission has been complied with.
1958–59	(267)	xvii	—— Chemical fertilisers.
1960–61	(218)	xix	—— Cigarettes and tobacco and cigarette and tobacco machinery.
1963–64	(21)	xvi	—— Electrical equipment for mechanically propelled land vehicles.
	(59)	xvi	—— Wallpaper.
1963–64	Cmnd.2299	xxvi	Monopolies, mergers and restrictive practices.
1960–61	Cmnd.1273	xix	Registrar of restrictive trading agreements. Rep. for the period 7 August 1956 to 31 December 1959. (See succeeding Reps. in sessions 1961–62, 1963–64 and 1966–67, covering period 1960–6).

11. Consumer Protection

1959–60	Cmnd.1011	xii	Consumer protection. Cttee. J. T. Molony, *Ch*. Interim Rep.
1961–62	Cmnd.1781	xii	—— Final Rep.
1964	Non-Parl.		Consumer Council. [1st] Ann. Rep. The Council. (See succeeding Ann. Reps.).

12. Company Law and Practice; Building Societies

1956–57	Cmnd.221	viii	Bankruptcy law and deeds of arrangement law amendment. Cttee. J. B. Blagden, *Ch*. Rep. (See Breviate II, pp. 184–5).
1958	Non-Parl.		—— Mins. of ev. Bd. of Trade.
1961–62	Cmnd.1749	xii	Company law. Cttee. Ld. Jenkins, *Ch*. Rep.
1960	Non-Parl.		—— Mins. of ev., 1st–4th days. Bd. of Trade.
1961	Non-Parl.		—— Mins. of ev., 5th–20th days.
1962	Non-Parl.		—— Index to rep. and mins. of ev.
1955–1964			Companies Act, 1948. Investigations. Reps. Bd. of Trade.
1955	Non-Parl.		—— Chinese Engineering & Mining Co. Ltd. K. W. Mackinnon.
1957	Non-Parl.		—— Gordon Hotels Ltd. A. M. S. Stevenson, D.V. House.
1959	Non-Parl.		—— Hide & Co. Ltd. N. J. Skelhorn, W. S. Carrington. Interim and Final Reps.
1960	Non-Parl.		—— General, London and Urban Properties Ltd. E. S. Fay.
1960	Non-Parl.		—— Wright Hamer Textiles Ltd. N. J. Skelhorn, W. S. Carrington.
1961	Non-Parl.		—— H. Jasper & Co. Ltd. N. Faulks.
1961	Non-Parl.		—— Pilot Assurance Co. Ltd. N. Faulks, R. K. Lochhead.

12. Company Law and Practice; Building Societies—*continued*

1961	Non-Parl.	—— Eglinton Hotels (Scotland) Ltd. J. O. M. Hunter, T. C. Currie.
1963	Non-Parl.	—— Milletts Holdings (St. Pauls) Ltd. R. M. Honeybone.
1964	Non-Parl.	—— Madingley Investments Ltd. M. K. Harrison-Hall, J. A. Robertson-Walker.
1964	Non-Parl.	—— F. M. S. Rubber Planters Estates Ltd. R. V. Cusack, E. R. Nicholson.
1964	Non-Parl.	—— Johore Para Rubber Co. Ltd. R. V. Cusack, E. R. Nicholson.
1964	Non-Parl.	—— Freehold Land Finance Co. Ltd. M. M. Wheeler, D. D. R. Smith. Interim and Final Reps.
1964	Non-Parl.	—— Majestic Insurance Co. Ltd. R. V. Cusack, E. R. Nicholson. Interim and Final Reps.
1958–1962		Building Societies Act, 1894. Reps. Registry of Friendly Societies.
1958	Non-Parl.	—— Blackpool Building Society. A. Vollmar.' Interim Rep.
1961	Non-Parl.	—— State Building Society (publ. as App. III to Pt. 5 of the ann. Rep. of the Chief Registrar for 1960.).
1961	Non-Parl.	—— Lloyds Permanent Building Society. D. Leigh. Interim Rep.
1962	Non-Parl.	—— —— Final Rep.

VI. COAL, FUEL, POWER, WATER

1. Coal

1955		Organisation. Nat. Coal Bd. Adv. Cttee. A. Fleck, *Ch.* Rep., apps. (not published by H.M.S.O.)
1956		Investing in coal. Progress and prospects under the Plan for Coal. Nat. Coal Bd. (not published by H.M.S.O.)
1955–56	Cmd.9747 xxxvi	Coal Industry Bill. [Raising limit of advances to N.C.B. from £350 mn. to £650 mn.] Memo. (See Breviate III, p. 181).
1957–58	(187–I) vi	Nationalised industries (Reports and Accounts) Sel. Cttee. T. A. R. W. Low. *Ch.* Rep., proc., mins. of ev., apps.
1957–58	Cmnd.415 xxiv	Capital investment in the coal, gas and electricity industries. (The first of four annual Papers. Information continued in Public investment in Great Britain, annual from session 1960–61 to 1963–64).
1959		Revised plan for coal. Progress of reconstruction and revised estimates of demand and output. Nat. Coal Bd. (not published by H.M.S.O.)
1959–60	Cmnd.895 xxvii	Coal Industry Bill [Increase of borrowing powers]. Memo.
1957	Non-Parl.	Clearances on transport roads in coal mines. Cttee. R. Yates, *Ch.* Rep., app. Min. of Power.

1. Coal—*continued*

1957–58	Cmnd.446	viii	Coal distribution costs in Great Britain. Cttee. T. B. Robson, *Ch*. Rep.
1959–60	Cmnd.999	ix	Solid smokeless fuels. Cttee. N. M. Peech, *Ch*. Rep.
1959–60	Cmnd.1120	ix	Coal derivatives. Cttee. A. H. Wilson, *Ch*. Rep.
1963–64	Cmnd.2231	xxvi	Domestic fuel supplies and the clean air policy.
1962	Non-Parl.		Scottish peat. Cttee. E. V. Appleton, *Ch*. 2nd Rep., apps. Dept. of Agric. & Fish., Scot. (see Breviate III, p. 183).

2. Electricity

1954–55	(HL.53)	iii	North Wales Hydro-Electric Power Bill. Sel. Cttee HL. Special Rep.
1958	Non-Parl.		Nuclear power station at Trawsfynydd. Inquiry. H. W. Grimmitt, C. D. Buchanan. Rep., apps. Min. of Power.
1955–56	Cmd.9672	xv	Electricity supply industry. Cttee. E. S. Herbert, *Ch*. Rep.
1956–57	Cmnd.27	xxvi	Electricity supply industry. Proposals for re-organisation.
1956–57	(304)	vii	Nationalised industries (Reports and Accounts). Sel. Cttee. P. Spens, *Ch*. Rep., proc., mins. of ev.
1957–58	Cmnd.415	xxiv	Capital investment in the coal, gas and electricity industries. (The first of four annual Papers. Information continued in Public investment in Great Britain, annual from session 1960–61 to 1963–64.).
1957	Non-Parl.		Nuclear generating station [Hunterston]. Inquiries. H. R. Leslie. Rep., apps. Scottish Home Dept.
1958–59	Cmnd.605	xvi	Methods adopted by the London Electricity Board for the disposal of scrap cable. Inquiry. H. Benson. Rep.
1958–59	Cmnd.618	xxv	Electricity (Borrowing Powers) Bill. Memo.
1958–59	Cmnd.695	xiii	Co-operation between area and Scottish electricity and gas boards. Cttee. C. M. Weir, *Ch*. Rep.
1958–59	(313)	xii	Central Electricity Generating Board. 1st Ann. Rep. & Accounts. (See Ann. Reps. p. 98).
1961–62	Cmnd.1564	xxxi	Electricity (Borrowing Powers) Order, 1961 and the Electricity (Borrowing Powers) (South of Scotland Electricity Board) Order, 1961. Memo.
1962–63	Cmnd.1859	xvii	Generation and distribution of electricity in Scotland. Cttee. C. H. Mackenzie, *Ch*. Rep.
1961–62	(269)	vii	Nationalised industries. Electricity supply industry. Sel. Cttee. G. R. H. Nugent, *Ch*. 2nd Special Rep., proc. (Formal only.).
1962–63	(236–I)	vi	—— Sel. Cttee. G. R. H. Nugent, *Ch*. Vol. I. Rep., proc.
	(236–II)	vii	—— —— Vol. II. Mins. of ev.
	(236–III)	vii	—— —— Vol. III. Apps., index.

2. Electricity—*continued*

1963–64 (67)	vii	—— Sel. Cttee. 1st Special Rep. Observations of the Electricity Council and the Minister of Power.
1963–64 Cmnd.2205	xxvi	Electricity and Gas Bill. Memo.

3. Gas

1957–58 Cmnd.415	xxiv	Capital investment in the coal, gas and electricity industries. (The first of four annual Papers. Information continued in Public investment in Great Britain, annual from session 1960–61 to 1963–64.).
1958–59 Cmnd.695	xiii	Co-operation between area and Scottish electricity and gas boards. Cttee. C. M. Weir, *Ch.* Rep.
1959–60 Cmnd.947	xxvii	Gas Bill. Memo.
1960–61 (280)	vii	Nationalised industries. Gas industry. Sel. Cttee. T. A. R. W. Low, *Ch.* Vol. I. Rep., proc.
(280–I)	vii	—— Vol. II. Mins. of ev., apps., index.
1961–62 (218)	vii	—— Sel. Cttee. Special Rep. Observations of the Gas Council and of the Minister of Power.
1963–64 (150)	vii	—— Sel. Cttee. 2nd Special Rep. Further observations of the Minister of Power.
1963–64 Cmnd.2205	xxvi	Electricity and Gas Bill. Memo.

4. Atomic Energy

1955–56 (95)	xi	U.K. Atomic Energy Authority. 1st Ann. Rep. (see Ann. Reps. p. 98).
1957–58 Cmnd.302	xxiv	Accident at Windscale no. 1 pile on 10th October, 1957. (Annex 1 & 11: Summary Reps. of U.K.A.E.A. Cttee., W. Penney, *Ch.*, on cause of the accident and measures taken to deal with it and its consequences. Annex III: Rep. of Medical Research Council Cttee., H. P. Himsworth, *Ch.*, on health and safety aspects.).
1957–58 Cmnd.338	vii	Organisation of certain parts of the U.K. Atomic Energy Authority. Cttee. A. Fleck, *Ch.* Rep., apps.
1957–58 Cmnd.342	vii	Organisation for control of health and safety in the U.K. Atomic Energy Authority. Cttee. A. Fleck, *Ch.* Rep.
1957–58 Cmnd.471	vii	Design and operation of the Windscale piles. Cttee. A. Fleck, *Ch.* Final Rep. (Interim Rep. not published.).
1960	Non-Parl.	Training in radiological health and safety. Cttee. D. Veale, *Ch.* Rep., apps. U.K. Atomic Energy Authority.
1957	Non-Parl.	Nuclear generating station [Hunterston]. Inquiries. H. R. Leslie. Rep., apps. Scottish Home Dept.
1958	Non-Parl.	Nuclear power station at Trawsfynydd. Inquiry. H. W. Grimmitt, C. D. Buchanan. Rep., apps. Min. of Power.
1959–60 Cmnd.884	xxvii	Control of radioactive waste.

4. Atomic Energy—*continued*

1959–60 Cmnd.1083 xxvii		Nuclear power programme.
1963–64 Cmnd.2335 xxvi		Second nuclear power programme.
1963–64 Cmnd.2358 viii		Nuclear power for ship propulsion. Working Group. J. Dunnett, T. Padmore, *Ch.* Rep.

5. Oil and Petrol

1959–60 (280)	iv	Esso Petroleum Company Bill. Sel. Cttee. J. S. W. Arbuthnot, *Ch.* Special Rep.
(281)	iv	—— Rep., proc.

6. Water

1959   Non-Parl.   Information on water resources. Central Adv. Cttee. Sub-Cttee. J. Proudman, *Ch.* Rep., apps. Min. of Housing & Local Govt.

1959   Non-Parl.   Growing demand for water. Central Adv. Cttee. Sub-Cttee. R. C. Yates, *Ch.* 1st Rep., apps. Min. of Housing & Local Govt.

1960   Non-Parl.   —— 2nd Rep. J. Proudman, *Ch.*

1962   Non-Parl.   —— Final Rep. J. Proudman, *Ch.*

1960–61 Cmnd.1331 xxi   Water resources of Wales. Welsh Adv. Cttee. L. O. Owen, *Ch.* Rep.

1961–62 Cmnd.1693 xxxi   Water conservation in England and Wales.

1963   Non-Parl.   Water resources in the North-West. Conference. Ld. Jellicoe, *Ch.* Rep., apps. Min. of Housing & Local Govt.

1963   Non-Parl.   Water service in central Scotland. Scottish Adv. Cttee. C. Mitchell, *Ch.* Rep., apps. Scottish Development Dept.

1963   Non-Parl.   Water charges. Central Adv. Cttee. Sub-Cttee. J. Cockram, *Ch.* Rep., apps. Min. of Housing & Local Govt.

1961   Non-Parl.   Pollution of water by tipped refuse. Technical Cttee. A. Key, *Ch.* Rep., app. Min. of Housing & Local Govt.

VII. TRANSPORT

1. General

1960   Unpublished   British Transport Commission. Adv. Group. I. A. R. Stedeford, *Ch.* Rep. (see H.C. Debates, 6/4/1960, cols. 393–9; Written answers 22/6/1960, cols. 47–8).

1960–61 Cmnd.1248 xxvii   Reorganisation of the nationalised transport undertakings. White Paper.

1962–63 (232)	xxv	British Transport Com. [Final] Ann. Rep. & Accounts ... 1962. Vol. I, Rep.
(232–I)	xxv	—— Vol. II. Financial and Statistical Accounts.

1963   Non-Parl.   Transport needs of Great Britain in the next twenty years. Group. R. L. Hall, *Ch.* Rep. Min. of Transport.

2. Railways

1955–56	Cmd.9880	xxxvi	British Transport Commission. Proposals for the railways. Statement and Memo. (See Breviate III, p. 199).
1956–57	Cmnd.262	xix	Purchasing procedure of the British Transport Commission. H. G. Howitt. Rep.
1957–58	Cmnd.360	xviii	Lewes-East Grinstead branch railway. Proposed withdrawal of train services. Central Transport Consultative Cttee. Ld. Coleraine, *Ch.* Rep.
1958–59	Cmnd.585	xxv	Minister of Transport and Civil Aviation and the Chairman of the British Transport Com. Exchange of correspondence.
1958–59	Cmnd.813	xix	Re-appraisal of the plan for the modernisation and re-equipment of British Railways. British Transport Com. B. H. Robertson, *Ch.* Rep. (See Breviate III, p. 199).
1959–60	(254)	vii	Nationalised industries. British Railways. Sel. Cttee. T. A. R. W. Low, *Ch.* Rep.
	(254–I)	vii	—— Rep., proc., mins. of ev., apps.
1960–61	(163)	vii	—— Observations of the B.T.C. and the Minister of Transport.
1960–61	Cmnd.1248	xxvii	Reorganisation of the nationalised transport undertakings. White Paper.
1963	Non-Parl.		Transport needs of Great Britain in the next twenty years. Group. R. L. Hall, *Ch.* Rep. Min. of Transport.
1963	Non-Parl.		Reshaping of British railways. British Railways Bd. R. Beeching, *Ch.* Pt. 1. Rep. Pt. 2. Maps. Min. of Transport.
1963–64	(233)	xix	British Railways Board. [1st] Ann. Rep. and Accounts. (See succeeding Ann. Reps.).
1961	Non-Parl.		Accidents . . . in Glasgow suburban electric trains in the Scottish Region British Railways. C. A. Langley. Interim Rep. Min. of Transport.
1961	Non-Parl.		—— 2nd Interim Rep. Accidents and failures . . . in multiple unit electric trains in the Scottish Region and Eastern Region British Railways.
1962	Non-Parl.		—— Final Rep.
1957–1961			British Transport Commission Charges Schemes. Min. of Transport & Civil Aviation. 1960: Min. of Transport.
1957	Non-Parl.		—— Railway Merchandise, 1957.
1957	Non-Parl.		—— Passenger, 1957.
1958	Non-Parl.		—— Inland Waterways, 1958.
1958	Non-Parl.		—— Railway Merchandise, 1957. Alterations . . . Jan., 1958.
1958	Non-Parl.		—— Harbours, 1958.
1959	Non-Parl.		—— Passenger, 1959. Interim decision, May, 1959.
1959	Non-Parl.		—— —— Confirmed by Order July, 1959.
1960	Non-Parl.		—— Hull Harbour, 1960.

2. Railways—*continued*

1960	Non-Parl.	—— Grimsby Harbour, 1960.
1960	Non-Parl.	—— Fleetwood Harbour, 1960.
1960	Non-Parl.	—— Lowestoft Harbour, 1960.
1961	Non-Parl.	—— Passenger, 1959. Alterations . . . June, 1961.

1964   Non-Parl.   London fares (British Railways) Order, 1963, London fares (London Transport) Order, 1963. Min. of Transport.

1964   Non-Parl.   —— Reasons for decision.

3. Inland Waterways

1957–58 Cmnd.486   xviii   Inland waterways. Cttee. H. L. Bowes, *Ch.* Rep.

1958–59 Cmnd.676   xxv   Inland waterways. Government proposals.

1958–59 (128)   vi   British Transport Commission. Petition for additional provision. Standing Orders Cttee. Special Rep.

1960–61 Cmnd.1248 xxvii   Reorganisation of the nationalised transport undertakings. White Paper.

1963–64 (232)   xix   British Waterways Board. [1st] Ann. Rep. and Accounts. (See succeeding Ann. Reps.).

1964   Non-Parl.   Future of the waterways. British Waterways Bd. J. M. K. Hawton, *Ch.* Interim Rep., app. The Board.

4. Roads, Road Traffic

1955–56 (410)   xxviii   Road Haulage Disposal Board. 7th and Final Rep. (See Breviate III, p. 198).

1960–61 Cmnd.1248 xxvii   Reorganisation of the nationalised transport undertakings. White Paper.

1963–64 (222)   xix   Transport Holding Company. [1st] Ann. Rep. and Accounts. (See succeeding Ann. Reps.).

1963   Non-Parl.   Transport needs of Great Britain in the next twenty years. Group. R. L. Hall, *Ch.* Rep. Min. of Transport.

1956   Non-Parl.   Child cyclists. Road Safety Cttee. H. Molson, *Ch.* Rep., app. Min. of Transport & Civil Aviation. (See Breviate III, p. 203).

1958   Non-Parl.   Child cyclists. Working Party. D. C. Haselgrove, *Ch.* Rep., apps. Min. of Transport & Civil Aviation.

1957   Non-Parl.   Minimum age for motor cyclists. Road Safety Cttee. G. R. H. Nugent, *Ch.* Rep., apps. Min. of Transport & Civil Aviation. (See Breviate III, p. 203).

1957   Non-Parl.   Road safety. The Slough experiment. Management Group. D. C. Haselgrove, *Ch.* Rep., apps., index. Min. of Transport & Civil Aviation.

1957–58 Cmnd.430   xxiv   Periodic vehicle tests. White Paper.

1959   Non-Parl.   Effect of small doses of alcohol on a skill resembling driving. G. C. Drew, H. A. Long, W. P. Colquhoun. Memo. 38. Medical Research Council.

4. Roads, Road Traffic—*continued*

1960	Non-Parl.		Road accidents—Christmas 1959. Road Research Technical Paper no. 49. D.S.I.R.
1964	Non-Parl.		Fatal road accidents at Christmas 1963. Road Research Technical Paper no. 72. D.S.I.R.
1959–60 (HL.26)		iv	Dogs. Papers relating to the number of road accidents in Great Britain in which dogs are the cause or a contributory cause and related matters.
1958–59 Cmnd.630		xvi	Consolidation of highway law. Cttee. Ld. Reading, *Ch.* Rep.
1958–59 (91–I)		vi	Highways Bill H.L. Jt. Sel. Cttee. Ld. Reading, *Ch.* Rep., proc., mins. of ev.
1962	Non-Parl.		Traffic signs for motorways. Adv. Cttee. C. S. Anderson, *Ch.* Final Rep., apps. (Interim Rep. not published.) Min. of Transport.
1963	Non-Parl.		Traffic signs. Cttee. W. J. Worboys, *Ch.* Rep., apps. Min. of Transport.
1964	Non-Parl.		Control of motor rallies. Adv. Cttee. Ld. Chesham, *Ch.* Rep., apps. Min. of Transport.
1959	Non-Parl.		Transport of goods by road. Sample Survey. Rep. Min. of Transport & Civil Aviation.
1964	Non-Parl.		Survey of road goods transport 1962. Final results, Pt. I. Min. of Transport.
1964	Non-Parl.		—— Pt. II. Commodity analysis.
1966	Non-Parl.		—— Pt. III. Methodological rep.
1966	Non-Parl.		—— Pt. IV. Geographical analysis.
1963	Non-Parl.		Traffic in towns. A study of the long term problems of traffic in urban areas. Steering Group, G. Crowther, *Ch.* and Working Group, C. D. Buchanan, *Ch.* Reps. Min. of Transport.
1964	Non-Parl.		Road pricing. The economic and technical possibilities. Panel. R. J. Smeed, *Ch.* Rep., apps. Min. of Transport.
1958	Non-Parl.		Roads in England and Wales. Rep. (See succeeding Ann. Reps. in Parliamentary series from 1958–59). Min. of Transport & Civil Aviation.
1960	Non-Parl.		London–Yorkshire motorway. 1st section. London–Birmingham. Min. of Transport.
1960	Non-Parl.		London–Birmingham motorway traffic and economics. Road Research Technical Paper no. 46. D.S.I.R.
1960	Non-Parl.		Ross motorway. Min. of Transport.
1964	Non-Parl.		American road construction plant. Investigation Team. Rep. Min. of Transport.
1955–56 Cmd.9741		xvii	Proposed underwater crossing of the Forth and the Forth road bridge scheme. Rep.

5. Rural Services

1961	Non-Parl.	Rural bus services. Cttee. D. T. Jack, *Ch.* Rep., apps. Min. of Transport.
1961	Non-Parl.	Design of roads in rural areas. Memo. Min. of Transport.
1963	Non-Parl.	Rural transport surveys. Rep. of preliminary results. Min. of Transport.
1961–62	Cmnd.1821 xxiv	Rural transport problem in Wales. Council for Wales & Monmouthshire. R. I. Aaron, *Ch.* Rep.
1961	Non-Parl.	Bus services in the Highlands and Islands. Highland Transport Enquiry. Ld. Cameron, C. J. D. Shaw, *Ch.* Rep., app. Min. of Transport.
1963	Non-Parl.	Transport services in the Highlands and Islands. Highland Transport Enquiry. Ld. Cameron, Ld. Kilbrandon, *Ch.* Rep., apps. Min. of Transport.
1962	Non-Parl.	Undertaking between the Sec. of State for Scotland and David Macbrayne Ltd. Dept. of Agric. & Fish., Scot.
1962	Non-Parl.	Undertaking between the Sec. of State for Scotland and the Orkney Islands Shipping Co. Dept. of Agric. & Fish., Scot.
1963	Non-Parl.	Undertaking between the Sec. of State for Scotland and . . . Messrs. Bremner & Co. . . . . Stromness, Orkney. Dept. of Agric. & Fish., Scot.

6. Sea Transport, Ports

1956	Non-Parl.	Ports efficiency. Cttee. E. H. Murrant, *Ch.* 3rd Rep., apps. Min. of Transport & Civil Aviation. (See Breviate III, pp. 208–9).
1960–61	Cmnd.1248 xxvii	Reorganisation of the nationalised transport undertakings. White Paper.
1961–62	Cmnd.1824 xx	Major ports of Great Britain. Cttee. Ld. Rochdale, *Ch.* Rep.
1963–64	(269) xix	British Transport Docks Board. [1st] Ann. Rep. & Accounts. (See succeeding Ann. Reps.).
1957	Non-Parl.	Carriage of dangerous goods and explosives in ships. Standing Adv. Cttee. H. E. Watts, *Ch.* Rep., apps., index. Min. of Transport & Civil Aviation.
1959–60	Cmnd.958 xix	Safety of nuclear-powered merchant ships. Cttee. ,P. Faulkner, *Ch.* Rep.
1963–64	Cmnd.2358 viii	Nuclear power for ship propulsion. Working Group. L. J. Dunnett, T. Padmore, *Ch.* Rep.
1960	Unpublished	Cunard. Replacement of the 'Queen' liners. Cttee. Ld. Chandos, *Ch.* Rep. (Rep. was confidential. For summary see H.C. Debates, 1/6/1960, cols. 1440–2; 3/11/1960, cols. 361–5.)
1960–61	Cmnd.1319 xxvii	Replacement of the 'Queen Mary'. Memo. of points of agreement between the Cunard Steam-Ship Co. Ltd. and H.M. Government.

6. Sea Transport, Ports—*continued*

1963	Non-Parl.	Shipping services to Northern Ireland. Cttee. D. V. House, *Ch*. Rep., apps. Min. of Transport.

7. Air Transport

1957–58	(304)	vi	Nationalised industries (Reports and Accounts). Sel. Cttee. T. A. R. W. Low, *Ch*. Special Rep., proc. [Formal only.]
1958–59	(213)	vii	—— Sel. Cttee. T. A. R. W. Low, *Ch*. Rep., Air Corporations, proc., mins. of ev., apps.
1959–60	(339)	vii	—— Sel. Cttee. Special Rep. Replies of the Air Corporations and comments of the Minister.
1963–64	(5)	xxvi	Financial problems of B.O.A.C. White Paper.
1963–64	(240)	vii	Nationalised industries. B.O.A.C. Sel. Cttee. G. R. H. Nugent, *Ch*. Vol. I. Rep., proc.
	(240–I)	vii	—— Vol. II. Mins. of ev., apps., index.
1957	Non-Parl.		London airport development. Cttee. P. E. Millbourn, *Ch*. Rep., apps. Min. of Transport & Civil Aviation.
1960–61	(281)	viii	Air Transport Licensing Board. [1st] Rep. (See succeeding Ann. Reps.).
1960–61	Cmnd.1457	xxvii	Civil aerodromes and air navigational services.
1961	Non-Parl.		Civil aircraft accident investigation and licence control. Cttee. D. A. S. Cairns, *Ch*. Rep., apps. Min. of Aviation.
1961–62	Cmnd.1695	xxxi	Aviation safety.
1961	Non-Parl.		Planning of helicopter stations in the London area. Cttee. G. I. Morris, *Ch*. Rep., apps. Min. of Aviation.
1963	Non-Parl.		Pilot training. Cttee. Duke of Hamilton, *Ch*. Rep., apps. Min. of Aviation.
1963	Non-Parl.		Air freight. Working Party. G. V. Hole, *Ch*. Rep., apps. Min. of Aviation.
1963–64	Cmnd.2428	xvi	Pricing of Ministry of Aviation contracts. Inquiry. J. G. Lang, *Ch*. 1st Rep.
1964–65	Cmnd.2581	xix	—— 2nd Rep.
1964	Non-Parl.		Third London airport. Inter-Dept. Cttee. G. V. Hole, *Ch*. Rep., apps. Min. of Aviation.

8. Channel Tunnel

1962–63	Cmnd.2137	ix	Proposals for a fixed Channel link. [Working Group. D. R. Serpell, J. Ravanel, *Ch*. Jt. Rep. on Proposals by the Channel Tunnel and Channel Bridge Study Groups.]

VIII. POST OFFICE, TELECOMMUNICATIONS, BROADCASTING, THE PRESS

1. Post Office, Telecommunications

1955–56	Cmd.9576	xxvi	Post Office development and finance. Rep.

1. Post Office, Telecommunications—*continued*

1957–58 Cmnd.303 xxiv	Full automation of the telephone system.
1957–58 Cmnd.318 xxiv	Post Office and Telegraph (Money). Memo. on proposed resolution.
1957–58 Cmnd.436 xxiv	Telephone policy. The next steps.
1958 Non-Parl.	Inland telegraph service. Adv. Cttee. L. Sinclair, *Ch.* Rep.
1958–59 Cmnd.690 xxv	Post Office capital expenditure 1959–60.
1959–60 Cmnd.973 xxvii	—— 1960–61.
1959–60 Cmnd.882 xxvii	Post Office and Telegraph (Money). Memo. on proposed resolution.
1959–60 Cmnd.989 xxvii	Status of the Post Office. White Paper.
1960–61 Cmnd.1247 xxvii	Post Office Bill. Memo.
1960–61 Cmnd.1327 xxvii	Post Office prospects 1961–62. (See succeeding Annuals).
1963–64 Cmnd.2211 xxvi	The inland telephone service in an expanding economy.
1963–64 Cmnd.2436 xxvi	Satellite communications.

2. Broadcasting, Mobile Radio

1954–55 Cmd.9451 xiii	Licence granted . . . by H. M. Postmaster General to the Independent Television Authority. (See Breviate III, p. 223).
1955–56 (288) vi	Broadcasting (Anticipation of Debates). Sel. Cttee. L. Heald, *Ch.* Rep., mins. of ev., etc.
1956–57 Cmnd.39 ix	Welsh broadcasting. Cttee. G. H. Ince, *Ch.* Rep.
1960 Non-Parl.	Television. Adv. Cttee. C. Daniel, *Ch.* Rep. Post Office.
1961–62 Cmnd.1536 xxxi	Draft of the Royal Charter for the continuance of the B.B.C.
1961–62 Cmnd.1537 xxxi	Copy of the licence and agreement dated Nov. 6, 1961, between H.M. Postmaster-General and the B.B.C.
1961–62 Cmnd.1724 xxxi	Copy of Royal Charter for the continuance of the B.B.C.
1961–62 Cmnd.1753 ix Cmnd.1819 ix Cmnd.1819–1 x	Broadcasting. Cttee. H. W. H. Pilkington, *Ch.* Rep. —— App. E, Vol. I, Memoranda. —— App. E, Vol. II, Memoranda.
1962 Non-Parl.	Future of sound radio and television. A short version of the Rep. of the Pilkington Cttee. Post Office.
1961–62 Cmnd.1770 xxxi	Broadcasting. Memo.
1962–63 Cmnd.1893 xxxi	Broadcasting. Further memo.
1963–64 Cmnd.2236 xxvi	Copy of the licence and agreement between H.M. Postmaster-General and the B.B.C.
1963–64 Cmnd.2237 xxvi	Draft of the Royal Charter for the continuance of the B.B.C.
1963–64 Cmnd.2385 xxvi	Copy of Royal Charter for the continuance of the

2. Broadcasting, Mobile Radio—*continued*

1963–64	Cmnd.2424	xxvi	Copy of the licence granted . . . to the Independent Television Authority.
1955	Non-Parl.		Mobile radio. Cttee. R. J. P. Harvey, *Ch.* 1st Rep., apps. Post Office.
1956	Non-Parl.		—— 2nd Rep., apps. W. A. Wolverson, *Ch.* (App. 1 contains Rep. of Sub-Cttee., H. S. Vian-Smith, *Ch.* on frequency sub-allocation; App. 2 contains Rep. of Sub-Cttee., R. L. Smith-Rose, *Ch.* on narrower channelling).
1959	Non-Parl.		—— 3rd Rep., apps. W. A. Wolverson, *Ch.* (App. 2 contains Rep. of Sub-Cttee., F. J. Smith, *Ch.* on allocation of 25 kc/s channels in low band).
1960	Non-Parl.		—— 4th Rep., apps. A. Wolstencroft, *Ch.*

3. The Press

1961–62	Cmnd.1811	xxi	The press. R. Com. Ld. Shawcross, *Ch.* Rep.
	Cmnd.1812	xxi	—— Mins. of oral ev. Vol. I.
	Cmnd.1812 –1	xxi	—— Mins. of oral ev. Vol. II.
	Cmnd.1812 –2	xxi	—— Mins. of oral ev. Vol. III.
	Cmnd.1812 –3	xxi	—— Index to mins. of oral ev.
	Cmnd.1812 –4 to –9	xxii	—— Documentary ev. Vols. I–VI.

IX. INVENTIONS, PATENTS

1955–56	Cmd.9744	xi	Awards to inventors. R.Com. Ld. Cohen, *Ch.* 4th and Final Rep. (See Breviate III, pp. 227–8).
1957	Non-Parl.		—— Use of inventions and designs by government departments. Compendium of principles and procedure adopted . . . in assessing compensation and making awards.
1955–56	Cmd.9788	xiv	Defence contracts [Power of the Crown to authorise the use of unpatented inventions, etc. in defence contracts]. Cttee. H. G. Howitt, *Ch.* Rep.

X. LABOUR

1. Manpower, Supply of Labour, Industrial Training

1955	Non-Parl.	Recruitment of scientists and engineers by the engineering industry. Adv. Council on Scientific Policy. Scientific Manpower Cttee. S. Zuckerman, *Ch.* Rep., apps. Ld. President's Office.
1956	Non-Parl.	Scientific and engineering manpower in Great Britain. Min. of Labour. Inquiry. Rep. and Adv. Council on Scientific Policy. Scientific Manpower Cttee. S. Zuckerman, *Ch.* Rep. Min. of Labour & N. S. and Ld. President's Office.

1. Manpower, Supply of Labour, Industrial Training—*continued*

1959–60 Cmnd.902 xx	Scientific and engineering manpower in Great Britain, 1959. Adv. Council on Scientific Policy. Scientific Manpower Cttee. S. Zuckerman, *Ch.* Rep.
1960–61 Cmnd.1490 xx	Long term demand for scientific manpower. Adv. Council on Scientific Policy. Scientific Manpower Cttee. S. Zuckerman, *Ch.* Memo. and Statistics Cttee. H. Campion, *Ch.* Rep.
1962–63 Cmnd.2146 xxiv	Scientific and technological manpower in Great Britain, 1962. Adv. Council on Scientific Policy. Scientific Manpower Cttee. S. Zuckerman, *Ch.* Rep.
1962	Manpower situation. Nat. Jt. Adv. Council. Working Party. C. J. Maston, *Ch.* Rep. (See Min. of Labour Gazette, Feb., 1962, pp. 45–9).
1959 Non-Parl.	Practices impeding the full and efficient use of manpower. Nat. Jt. Adv. Council. Inquiry. Rep., apps. Min. of Labour & N.S.
1956 Non-Parl.	Automation. Technical trends and their impact on management and labour. Rep. D.S.I.R.
1955–56 Cmd.9628 xvii	Employment of older men and women. Nat. Adv. Cttee. H. A. Watkinson, *Ch.* 2nd Rep. (See Breviate III, p. 262).
1958–59 Cmnd.789 viii	Resettlement Advisory Board [for those retired from the Regular Armed Forces]. F. C. Hooper, *Ch.* Progress Rep., 1957–9.
1957 Non-Parl.	Building apprenticeship and training council. F. W. Leggett, *Ch.* Final Rep., apps. Min. of Works. (See Breviate III, pp. 250–1).
1958 Non-Parl.	Training for skill. Recruitment and training of young workers in industry. Nat. Jt. Adv. Council. Sub-Cttee. L. R. Carr, *Ch.* Rep. Min. of Labour & N.S.
1962–63 Cmnd.1892 xxxi	Industrial training: government proposals.
1962 Non-Parl.	Selection and training of supervisors. Cttee. D. C. Barnes, *Ch.* Rep., apps. Min. of Labour. (See Breviate III, p. 239).
1964 Non-Parl.	—— Progress Rep. A. S. Marre, *Ch.*

2. Cost of Living. Wages and Incomes Policy

1955–56 Cmd.9725 xxxvi	Economic implications of full employment. (See Breviate III, pp. 235–6).
1956 Non-Parl.	Studies in urban household diets, 1944–49. Nat. Food Survey Cttee. N. C. Wright, *Ch.* 2nd Rep., apps., index. (See Breviate III, p. 90, and Domestic food consumption and expenditure. Nat. Food Survey Cttee. Ann. Reps. Non-Parl.).
1957 Non-Parl.	Household expenditure, 1953–54. Enquiry. Rep. Min. of Labour & N.S.
1961 Non-Parl.	Family expenditure survey. Rep. for 1957–59. Min. of Labour. (See Rep. for 1960 and 1961; 1962 Non-Parl., and succeeding Ann. Reps.).

2. Cost of Living. Wages and Incomes Policy—*continued*

1955–56 Cmd.9710 xiii		Proposals for a new index of retail prices. Cost of Living Adv. Cttee. W. J. Neden, *Ch.* Rep.
1961–62 Cmnd.1657 xii		Revision of the index of retail prices. Cost of Living Adv. Cttee. P. H. St. J. Wilson, *Ch.* Rep.
1958 Non-Parl.		Prices, productivity and incomes. Council. Ld. Cohen, *Ch.* 1st Rep.
1958 Non-Parl.		—— 2nd Rep.
1959 Non-Parl.		—— 3rd Rep.
1961 Non-Parl.		—— 4th Rep. Ld. Heyworth, *Ch.*
1961–62 Cmnd.1626 xxxi		Incomes policy: the next step.
1962–63 Cmnd.1844 xxxi		National Incomes Commission. White Paper.
		National Incomes Com. F. G. Lawrence, *Ch.* Reps.
1962–63 Cmnd.1994 xxi		—— Scottish plumbers' and Scottish builders' agreements of 1962.
Cmnd.2098 xxi		—— Rep. no. 2. Agreements in electrical contracting.
1963–64 Cmnd.2317 xvii		—— Rep. no. 3. Remuneration of academic staff in universities and colleges of advanced technology.
Cmnd.2380 xvii		—— Rep. no. 4 (Interim). Agreements of Nov.–Dec. 1963 in the engineering and shipbuilding industries.
1964–65 Cmnd.2583 xix		—— Rep. no. 4 (Final).

3. Industrial Relations

i. Wages Councils, Truck, Holidays

1956 Non-Parl.		Establishment of a wages council for the rubber proofed garment making industry. Com. H. S. Kirkaldy, *Ch.* Rep., apps. Min. of Labour & N.S.
1961 Non-Parl.		Sugar confectionery and food preserving wages council. Com. G. G. Honeyman, *Ch.* Rep., app. Min. of Labour.
1963 Non-Parl.		Baking wages council (Scotland). Com. H. S. Kirkaldy, *Ch.* Rep., apps. Min. of Labour.
1964 Non-Parl.		Licensed residential establishment and licensed restaurant wages council. Com. J. G. Picton, *Ch.* Rep., apps. Min. of Labour.
1957 Non-Parl.		Agricultural Wages Act, 1948. Rep. of proceedings . . . for the period Oct. 1, 1950–Sept. 30, 1955. Min. of Agric., Fish. & Food. (See Safety, health, welfare and wages in agriculture. Ann. Reps. 1962 onwards. Non-Parl.).
1961 Non-Parl.		Truck Acts. Cttee. D. Karmel, *Ch.* Rep., apps. Min. of Labour.
1962–63 Cmnd.2105 xxxi		Staggered holidays.

ii. Disputes

1954–55 Cmd.9352 v		Dispute between the British Transport Commission and the National Union of Railwaymen. Ct. of Inquiry. Ld. Cameron (J. Cameron), *Ch.* Interim Rep.
Cmd.9372 v		—— Final Rep.

3. Industrial Relations—*continued*

1954–55 Cmd.9439 v	Dispute between members of the Newspaper Proprietors' Association and members of the Amalgamated Engineering Union and Electrical Trades Union. Ct. of Inquiry. J. Forster, *Ch.* Rep.
1955–56 Cmd.9717 xxi	Disputes between the London Master Printers' Association and the London Typographical Society and the Association of the Correctors of the Press. Ct. of Inquiry. J. Forster, *Ch.* Rep.
1957–58 Cmnd.510 xv	Dispute between employers who are members of the employers' side and workpeople who are represented on the workpeople's side of the National Joint Council for the Port Transport Industry. Ct. of Inquiry. Ld. Cameron (J. Cameron), *Ch.* Rep.
1960 Non-Parl.	Ocean shipowners' tally clerks. Cttee. H. Lloyd-Williams, *Ch.* Rep. Min. of Labour.
1964 Non-Parl.	Difference over the appointment of dock foremen at Southampton docks, Oct. 19, 1964. Inquiry. A. D. Flanders. Rep. Min. of Labour.
1955–56 Cmd.9843 xxi	Dispute between the Iron and Steel Trades Employers' Association and the National Joint Trade Unions' Craftsmen's Iron and Steel Committee. Ct. of Inquiry. J: Stewart, *Ch.* Rep.
1956–57 Cmnd.159 xiv	Dispute between employers who are members of the Engineering and Allied Employers' National Federation and workmen who are members of trade unions affiliated to the Confederation of Shipbuilding and Engineering Unions. Ct. of Inquiry. D. T. Jack, *Ch.* Rep.
1956–57 Cmnd.160 xiv	Dispute between employers who are members of the Shipbuilding Employers' Federation and workmen who are members of trade unions affiliated to the Confederation of Shipbuilding and Engineering Unions. Ct. of Inquiry. D. T. Jack, *Ch.* Rep.
1956–57 Cmnd.105 xiv	Dispute between B.O.A.C. and the Merchant Navy and Airline Officers' Association. Ct. of Inquiry. D. T. Jack. *Ch.* Rep.
1958–59 Cmnd.608 xvi	Dispute at London airport. Ct. of Inquiry. D. T. Jack, *Ch.* Rep.
1956–57 Cmnd.131 xiv	Dispute at Briggs Motor Bodies Ltd., Dagenham. Ct. of Inquiry. Ld. Cameron (J. Cameron), *Ch.* Rep.
1962–63 Cmnd.1999 xx	Dispute between the Ford Motor Co. Ltd. of Dagenham and members of the trade unions on the trade union side of the Ford National Joint Negotiating Committee. Ct. of Inquiry. D. T. Jack, *Ch.* Rep.
1963–64 Cmnd.2361 xv	Dispute between the parties represented on the National Joint Industrial Council for the electricity supply industry. Ct. of Inquiry. C. H. Pearson, *Ch.* Rep.

3. Industrial Relations—*continued*

1963–64 Cmnd.2202 viii   Complaint made by the National Union of Bank Employees to the Committee on Freedom of Association of the International Labour Organisation. Inquiry. Ld. Cameron (J. Cameron). Rep.

1964   Non-Parl.   Dispute at the Spitalfields, Borough, Stratford, Brentford and King's Cross Markets. Cttee. D. T. Jack, *Ch*. Rep., app. Min. of Labour.

1964   Non-Parl.   Difference existing in the Yorkshire Area of the coal-mining industry involving members of the Yorkshire Winding Enginemen's Association and members of the National Union of Mineworkers employed by the National Coal Board, and the National Coal Board. Cttee. R. M. Wilson, *Ch*. Rep. Min. of Labour.

4. Wages and Conditions in Particular Employments (other than Wages Councils)

1958   Non-Parl.   Smithfield market [industrial unrest arising from arrangements in the market]. Cttee. R. M. Wilson, *Ch*. Rep. Min. of Labour & N.S.

1959   Non-Parl.   Lister v. The Romford Ice and Cold Storage Co. Ltd. [legal decisions on liability of workers for injury]. Inter-Dept. Cttee. P. H. St. J. Wilson, *Ch*. Rep., app. Min. of Labour & N.S.

1955–56 Cmd.9813   xxvi   Operation of the Dock Workers (Regulation of Employment) Scheme, 1947. Cttee. P. A. Devlin, *Ch*. Rep.

1959   Non-Parl.   Cold store undertakings. Inquiry held under paras. 1(4) and (5) of the Schedule to the Dock Workers (Regulation of Employment) Act, 1946 [application of the scheme to cold store workers]. H. Lloyd-Williams. Rep. Min. of Labour & N.S.

1960   Non-Parl.   I. List of ports. II. Timber and pitwood. Inquiry held under paras. 1(4) and (5) of the schedule to the Dock Workers (Regulation of Employment) Act, 1946. H. Lloyd-Williams. Rep., app. Min. of Labour.

1960   Non-Parl.   Ocean shipowners' tally clerks. Cttee. H. Lloyd-Williams, *Ch*. Rep. Min. of Labour.

1961   Non-Parl.   Objections made to the Draft Dock Workers (Regulation of Employment) (Amendment) Order, 1961. Inquiry. Ld. Forster (J. Forster). Rep., app. Min. of Labour.

1964   Non-Parl.   Difference over the appointment of dock foremen at Southampton docks, Oct. 19, 1964. Inquiry. A. D. Flanders. Rep. Min. of Labour.

1963   Non-Parl.   Pay and conditions of employment of the drivers and conductors of the London Transport Board's road services. Cttee. E. H. Phelps Brown, *Ch*. Interim Rep. Min. of Labour.

1964   Non-Parl.   —— Rep., apps.

4. Wages and Conditions in Particular Employments—*continued*

1964	Non-Parl.	Pay of postmen. Cttee. A. Ll. Armitage, *Ch.* Rep., app. Treasury.
1964	Non-Parl.	—— Mins. of ev., apps.

5. Rehabilitation, Resettlement

1955–56 Cmd.9883	xiv	Rehabilitation, training and resettlement of disabled persons. Cttee. Ld. Piercy, *Ch.* Rep.
1958	Non-Parl.	Rehabilitation and resettlement of disabled persons. Standing Cttee. Dame M. G. Smieton, *Ch.* 3rd Rep. Min. of Labour & N. S. (See Breviate III, p. 261).
1957	Non-Parl.	Rehabilitation of amputees. Sub-Cttee., R. L. Kelham, *Ch.*, of Brussels Treaty Organisation (now Western European Union). Memo. on general principles. Min. of Health.
1962	Non-Parl.	Workshops for the blind. Working Party. J. G. Stewart, *Ch.* Rep., apps. Min. of Labour.

6. Young People

1955–56 Cmd.9738	xvii	Employment of children in the potato harvest. Cttee. H. Rose, *Ch.* Rep.
1957	Non-Parl.	Building apprenticeship and training council. F. W. Leggett, *Ch.* Final Rep., apps. Min. of Works. (See Breviate III, pp. 250–1).
1958	Non-Parl.	Training for skill. Recruitment and training of young workers in industry. Nat. Jt. Adv. Council. Sub-Cttee. L. R. Carr, *Ch.* Rep. Min. of Labour & N.S.
1961	Non-Parl.	Employment and training of young people, April 1959 —October 1961. Nat. Youth Employment Council. Ld. Coleraine, *Ch.* Interim Rep., apps. Min. of Labour.
1962	Non-Parl.	Work of the Youth Employment Service, 1959–62. Nat. Youth Employment Council. Ld. Coleraine, *Ch.* Rep., app. Min. of Labour.
1962–63 Cmnd.1892 xxxi		Industrial training: government proposals.

7. Safety and Health

1956	Non-Parl.	Industrial accident prevention. Nat. Jt. Adv. Council. Sub-Cttee. Dame M. G. Smieton, *Ch.* Rep. Min. of Labour & N.S.
1956	Non-Parl.	Conditions in iron foundries. Jt. Standing Cttee. T. W. McCullough, *Ch.* 1st Rep., apps. Min. of Labour & N.S.
1957	Non-Parl.	Safety, health and welfare conditions in non-ferrous foundries. Jt. Standing Cttee. R. Bramley-Harker, *Ch.* 1st Rep., apps. Min. of Labour & N.S.
1959	Non-Parl.	—— 2nd Rep. Technical Sub-Cttee. A. Graham, *Ch.* Rep.

7. Safety and Health—*continued*

1961	Non-Parl.	Conditions in steel foundries. Jt. Standing Cttee. H. Woods, *Ch.* 1st Rep., apps. Min. of Labour.
1964	Non-Parl.	Foundry goggles. Jt. Adv. Cttee. H. Woods, *Ch.* Rep. apps. Min. of Labour. (Apps. contain reps. of Sub-Cttee. apptd. by Jt. Adv. Cttee.).
1957	Non-Parl.	Safety in the use of power presses. Jt. Standing Cttee. T. W. McCullough, *Ch.* 3rd Rep. of proc., apps. Min. of Labour & N.S. (See Breviate III, p. 273).
1959	Non-Parl.	—— 4th Rep. of proc. R. Bramley-Harker, *Ch.* (Annex 1 contains Rep. of Sub-Cttee. on Methods of press control.).
1957	Non-Parl.	Dust in card rooms. Jt. Adv. Cttee. of the Cotton Industry. Miss A. S. Bettenson, *Ch.* 3rd Interim Rep. Min. of Labour & N.S. (See Breviate III, p. 269).
1960	Non-Parl.	—— 4th Interim Rep.
1961	Non-Parl.	—— Final Rep.
1958–59	Cmnd.558 xiii	Industrial health. Chief Inspector of Factories. [1st] Ann. Rep. (See Ann. Reps., p. 98).
1958	Non-Parl.	Industrial health. A survey of Halifax. Rep. by H.M. Factory Inspectorate and Recommendations of the Industrial Health Adv. Cttee. I. N. Macleod, *Ch.* Min. of Labour & N.S.
1959	Non-Parl.	Industrial health. A survey of the pottery industry in Stoke-on-Trent. H.M. Factory Inspectorate. Rep., apps. Min. of Labour & N.S.
1963	Non-Parl.	Dust control in potteries. Jt. Standing Cttee. Miss M. Brand, *Ch.* 1st Rep., apps. Min. of Labour.
1959–60	Cmnd.953 ix	Safety and health in the building and civil engineering industries 1954–1958. Rep.
1959–60	Cmnd.1173 xiv	Examination of steam boilers in industry. Adv. Cttee. G. G. Honeyman, *Ch.* Rep.
1960	Non-Parl.	Wool textile industry. Spacing of machinery. Minimum standards recommended by the Jt. Factory Adv. Cttee. and the Jt. Standing Cttee. Min. of Labour.
1961	Non-Parl.	Draft Construction (Lifting Operations) Regulations and the Construction (General Provisions) Regulations. Inquiry. G. G. Honeyman. Rep., apps. Min. of Labour.
1962	Non-Parl.	Safety, health, welfare and wages in agriculture. [1st] Ann. Rep. Min. of Agric., Fish. & Food. (See succeeding Ann. Reps.).
1964	Non-Parl.	Safety in paper mills. Jt. Standing Cttee. H. Woods, *Ch.* 1st Rep., apps. Min. of Labour.

8. Migration

1953–54	Cmd.9261 xviii	Oversea Migration Board. 1st Ann. Rep. (see succeeding Ann. Reps. up to session 1961–62, and annual Statistics from session 1962–63 to 1965–66).

8. Migration—continued

1955–56 Cmd.9832   xxiii   Child migration to Australia. Fact-finding Mission. J. Ross, Ch. Rep.

1961–62 Cmnd.1640 xxx   Commonwealth Immigrants Bill. Draft instructions to Immigration Officers.

1961–62 Cmnd.1716 xxx   Commonwealth Immigrants Act, 1962. Instructions to Immigration Officers.

1962–63 Cmnd.2119 x   Commonwealth Immigrants Advisory Council. [1st] Rep. (See succeeding Ann. Reps. up to session 1964–65, when Council superseded by Nat. Cttee. for Commonwealth Immigrants).

1962–63 Cmnd.2151 xxx   Commonwealth Immigrants Act, 1962. Control of immigration. Statistics for July 1962–June 1963. (See succeeding annual publications).

9. Professions

Items appearing in this section are either those dealing with the professions generally or those which have not been classified elsewhere.

For the medical professions, including medical practitioners, dentists, nurses, hospital administrators, pharmacists, etc., see Health, pp. 70–1 and pp. 69–70. For reports on school teachers, university teachers and librarians see Education, pp. 79–81, and p. 83. Reports on scientific and technological manpower will be found in Labour, pp. 59–60. The report on probation officers is in Legal Administration, p. 88.

1959–60 Cmnd.1033 xvii   Powers of subpoena of disciplinary tribunals. Dept. Cttee. Ld. Simonds, Ch. Rep.

1963–64 Cmnd.2430 xx   Recruitment for the veterinary profession. Dept. Cttee. Duke of Northumberland, Ch. Rep.

XI. SOCIAL SECURITY

1. National Insurance

1957–58 Cmnd.294   xv   National Insurance Bill, 1957. Govt. Actuary. Rep. on financial provisions.

1957–58 Cmnd.295   xxiv   Proposed changes in the national insurance schemes.

1958–59 Cmnd.629   xvi   National Insurance Bill, 1959. Govt. Actuary. Rep. on financial provisions.

1959–60 (220)   xvii   National Insurance Acts, 1946 to 1959. Govt. Actuary. Rep. on 2nd quinquennial review. (See Breviate III, pp. 295–6).

1959–60 (227)   xvii   National Insurance Acts, 1946 to 1959. Minister of Pensions & N.I. Rep. on his quinquennial review of the rates and amounts of the national insurance benefit.

1960–61 Cmnd.1196 xxvii   Proposed changes in the national insurance schemes.

1960–61 Cmnd.1197 xviii   National Insurance Bill, 1960. Govt. Actuary. Rep. on the financial provisions.

1962–63 Cmnd.1934 xxxi   Proposed changes in the national insurance schemes.

1962–63 Cmnd.1935 xx   National Insurance Bill, 1963. Govt. Actuary. Rep. on the financial provisions.

1. National Insurance—*continued*

1955–1964		National Insurance Adv. Cttee. W. Spens, *Ch.* to 1956. B. I. Evans, *Ch.* 1957 onwards. Reps. (See Breviate III, pp. 292–5).
1955–56	Cmd.9609 xxii	—— Benefit for very short spells of unemployment or sickness.
	Cmd.9684 xxii	—— Widow's benefits.
	Cmd.9752 xxii	—— Earnings limits for benefits.
	Cmd.9854 xxii	—— Contribution conditions and credits provisions.
	Cmd.9855 xxii	—— Dependency provisions.
1956–57	Cmnd.33 xv	—— Death grant question.
	Cmnd.206 xv	—— Part-time employment.
1959–60	Cmnd.964 xvii	—— Long-term hospital patients.
	Cmnd.1021 xvii	—— Doctors' and midwives' certificates for national insurance purposes.
1963–64	Cmnd.2400 xv	—— Time limits for claiming sickness benefit.
1964	Non-Parl.	Sick pay schemes. Nat. Jt. Adv. Council. Cttee. A. S. Marre, *Ch.* Rep., apps. Min. of Labour.
1964	Non-Parl.	Incidence of incapacity for work. Enquiry. Rep. Pt. I. Scope and characteristics of employers' sick pay schemes. Min. of Pensions & N.I.
1966	Non-Parl.	—— Pt. II. Incidence of incapacity for work in different areas and occupations. Min. of Social Security.

2. National Assistance

1954–55	Cmd.9334 xiii	Draft National Assistance (Determination of Need) Amendment Regulations, 1954. Memo.
1955–56	Cmd.9635 xxxvi	—— 1955. Memo.
1957–58	Cmnd.296 xxiv	—— 1957. Memo.
1958–59	Cmnd.782 xxv	Improvements in national assistance.
1960–61	Cmnd.1198 xxvii	Draft National Assistance (Determination of Need) Amendment Regulations, 1960. Memo.
1961–62	Cmnd.1768 xxxi	—— 1962. Memo.
1962–63	Cmnd.1943 xxxi	—— 1963. Memo.

3. Industrial Injuries

1955–56	Cmd.9548 xxii	Diseases provisions of the National Insurance (Industrial Injuries) Act. Dept. Cttee. F. W. Beney, *Ch.* Rep.
1956–1964		Industrial Injuries Adv. Council. A. Plant, *Ch.* Reps.
1955–56	Cmd.9673 xxii	—— Byssinosis.
1959–60	Cmnd.1095 xvii	—— Occupational cover in respect of byssinosis within the cotton industry.
1955–56	Cmd.9674 xxii	—— Cadmium poisoning.
	Cmd.9827 xxii	—— Rules governing assessment of disablement in cases involving damage to an organ which, in a normal person, is one of a pair.
1957–58	Cmnd.416 xv	—— Review of prescribed diseases schedule.
1963–64	Cmnd.2403 xv	—— Farmer's lung.
1959–60	(300) xvii	National Insurance (Industrial Injuries) Acts, 1946 to 1959. Govt. Actuary. Rep. on the 2nd quinquennial review. (See Breviate III, p. 300).

4. Pensions

1958	Non-Parl.	Occupational pension schemes. Govt. Actuary, ·G. H. Maddex. Survey.
1957–58	Cmnd.538 xxiv	Provision for old age. The future development of the national insurance scheme.

XII. HEALTH

1. National Health Service: General

1955–56	Cmd.9663 xx	Cost of the National Health Service. Cttee. C. W. Guillebaud, *Ch.* Rep.
1959	Non-Parl.	National Health Service Superannuation Scheme, 1948–55. Government Actuary. G. H. Maddex. Rep., apps. Min. of Health.
1959	Non-Parl.	—— Scotland, 1948–55. Government Actuary. G. H. Maddex. Rep., apps. Dept. of Health, Scot.
1958	Non-Parl.	Cost of prescribing. Cttee. A. H. S. Hinchliffe, *Ch.* Interim Rep. Min. of Health.
1959	Non-Parl.	—— Final Rep.
1959	Non-Parl.	Prescribing costs. Cttee. J. B. Douglas, *Ch.* Rep., apps. Dept. of Health, Scot.
1959	Non-Parl.	Classification of proprietary preparations. Standing Jt. Cttee. Ld. Cohen of Birkenhead, *Ch.* Rep. Min. of Health.
1960	Non-Parl.	—— Rep. Definition of drugs.
1961	Non-Parl.	—— Rep. Classification in category S.

2. Hospitals: Plans, Organisation, Staffing

1955	Non-Parl.	Hospital costing. Working Party. W. O. Chatterton, *Ch.* Rep., apps. Min. of Health.
1955–56	Cmd.9516 xxi	Hospital endowments. Com. S. A. Smith, *Ch.* Rep.
1961–62	Cmnd.1604 xxxi	Hospital plan for England and Wales.
1963	Non-Parl.	—— Revision to 1972–3. Min. of Health.
1964	Non-Parl.	—— Revision to 1973–4.
1961–62	Cmnd.1602 xxxi	Hospital plan for Scotland.
1964	Non-Parl.	—— Revision to 1973–4. Scottish Home & Health Dept.
1961	Non-Parl.	Special hospitals [Broadmoor, Rampton, Moss Side]. Working Party. D. Emery, *Ch.* Rep., app. Min. of Health.
1955	Non-Parl.	Hospital pharmaceutical service. Standing Adv. Cttee. Sub-Cttee. H. N. Linstead, *Ch.* Rep., apps. Min. of Health.
1956	Non-Parl.	Anaesthetic explosions, including safety code for equipment and installations. Working Party. G. Stead, *Ch.* Rep., apps., index. Min. of Health.

2. Hospitals: Plans, Organisation, Staffing—*continued*

1958	Non-Parl.	Control of dangerous drugs and poisons in hospitals. Standing Adv. Cttees. Jt. Sub-Cttee. Miss J. K. Aitken, *Ch.* Rep., apps. Min. of Health.
1959	Non-Parl.	Staphylococcal infections in hospitals. Standing Adv. Cttee. Sub-Cttee. Ld. Cohen of Birkenhead, *Ch.* Reps., apps. Min. of Health.
1962	Non-Parl.	Accident and emergency services. Standing Adv. Cttee. Sub-Cttee. H. Platt, *Ch.* Rep., apps. Min. of Health.
1962	Non-Parl.	Emergency treatment in hospital of cases of acute poisoning. Standing Adv. Cttee. Sub-Cttee. H. J. B. Atkins, *Ch.* Rep., apps. Min. of Health.
1959	Non-Parl.	Welfare of children in hospital. Cttee. H. Platt, *Ch.* Rep., app. Min. of Health.
1961	Non-Parl.	Pattern of the in-patient's day. Standing Adv. Cttee. Sub-Cttee. Miss M. B. Powell, *Ch.* Rep., apps. Min. of Health.
1962	Non-Parl.	Visiting patients in hospital. Cttee. J. Dunlop, *Ch.* Rep., apps. Scottish Home & Health Dept.
1959	Non-Parl.	Convalescent treatment. Working Party. N. M. Goodman, *Ch.* Rep., apps. Min. of Health.
1957	Non-Parl.	Hospital supplies. Cttee. F. Messer, *Ch.* Interim Rep. Min. of Health.
1958	Non-Parl.	—— Final Rep., apps.
1960	Non-Parl.	Hospital laundry arrangements. Cttee. Ld. Cunliffe, *Ch.* Rep. Min of Health.
1962	Non-Parl.	Hospital catering. Standing Adv. Cttees. Jt. Cttee. C. S. Gumley, *Ch.* Rep., apps. Dept. of Health, Scot.
1962	Non-Parl.	Hospital catering. Min. of Health.
1957	Non-Parl.	Grading structure of administrative and clerical staff in the hospital service. N. F. Hall. Rep., apps. Min. of Health.
1957	Non-Parl.	Medical superintendents and medical staff committees. Standing Adv. Cttee. Sub-Cttee. G. H. Henderson, *Ch.* Rep., apps. Dept. of Health, Scot.
1961	Non-Parl.	Medical staffing structure in the hospital service. Jt. Working Party. R. Platt, *Ch.* Rep., apps. Min. of Health.
1964	Non-Parl.	Medical staffing structure in Scottish hospitals. Cttee. J. H. Wright, *Ch.* Rep., apps. Scottish Home & Health Dept.
1962	Non-Parl.	Work, grading, training and qualifications of hospital engineers. Study Group. L. N. Tyler, *Ch.* Rep., apps. Min. of Health.

2. Hospitals: Plans, Organisation, Staffing—*continued*

1963   Non-Parl.   Recruitment, training and promotion of administrative
                                   and clerical staff in the hospital service. Cttee.
                                   E. S. L. Green, *Ch.* Rep., apps. Min. of Health.

3. Medical Professions

i. Medical Practitioners

1957   Non-Parl.   Future numbers of medical practitioners and the ap-
                                   propriate intake of medical students. Cttee. H.
                                   U. Willink, *Ch.* Rep., apps. Min. of Health.

1955–56 Cmd.9861   xiv   Recruitment to the dental profession. Cttee. Ld.
                                   McNair, *Ch.* Rep.

1959–60 Cmnd.939   xii   Doctors' and dentists' remuneration. R.Com. H. W.
                                   H. Pilkington, *Ch.* Rep.
        Cmnd.1064 xii   —— Supplement. Further statistical app.
1958   Non-Parl.   —— Mins. of ev., 1st–20th days.
1959   Non-Parl.   —— Mins. of ev., 21st–23rd days.
1960   Non-Parl.   —— —— App. to mins. of ev.
1957   Non-Parl.   —— Written ev., Vol. I.
1960   Non-Parl.   —— Written ev., Vol. II.
1961   Non-Parl.   —— Index to ev.

1963, 1965   Doctors' and dentists' remuneration. Review Body.
                                   1st and 2nd Reps. (See H. C. Debates, 25/3/63
                                   and 1/2/65).

1963   Non-Parl.   Field of work of the family doctor. Standing Adv.
                                   Cttee. Sub-Cttee. A. C. Gillie, *Ch.* Rep., apps.
                                   Min. of Health.

ii. Medical Auxiliaries; Nurses

1961–62 (HL.38)   v   Papers relating to qualified dieticians. occupational
                                   therapists, physiotherapists and radiographers
                                   in the National Health Service.

1955   Non-Parl.   State enrolled assistant nurse in the National Health
                                   Service. Standing Adv. Cttee. Sub–Cttee. Miss
                                   E. G. Manners, *Ch.* Rep. Dept. of Health, Scot.
                                   (See Breviate III, p. 327).

1955   Non-Parl.   Work of nurses in hospital wards. Standing Adv. Cttee.
                                   Sub-Cttee. Miss E. G. Manners, *Ch.* Rep., apps.
                                   Dept. of Health, Scot. (App. A is Rep. of Sub-
                                   Cttee. on Shortened forms of training).

1955   Non-Parl.   Training of district nurses. Working Party. I. F.
                                   Armer, *Ch.* Rep., apps. Min. of Health.

1959   Non-Parl.   Training of district nurses. Adv. Cttee. D. H. Ingall,
                                   Ch. Rep., apps. Min. of Health.

1959   Non-Parl.   Design of nurses' uniforms. Standing Adv. Cttee.
                                   Sub-Cttee. Miss K. G. Douglas, Miss M. J.
                                   Smyth, *Ch.* Rep., apps. Min. of Health.

1963   Non-Parl.   Experimental nurse training at Glasgow Royal In-
                                   firmary. Assessment Cttee. J. H. F. Brotherston,
                                   Ch. Rep., apps. Scottish Home & Health Dept.

3. Medical Professions—*continued*

1963	Non-Parl.	Communication between doctors, nurses and patients. An aspect of human relations in the hospital service. Standing Adv. Cttees. Jt. Sub-Cttee. Ld. Cohen of Birkenhead, *Ch.* Rep. Min. of Health.

iii. Other Services

1958	Non-Parl.	Organisation of laboratory services. Cttee. J. Dunlop, *Ch.* Rep., apps. Dept. of Health, Scot.
1956	Non-Parl.	Health visiting. Working Party. W. W. Jameson, *Ch.* Rep., apps., index. Min. of Health.
1959	Non-Parl.	Social workers in the local authority health and welfare services. Working Party. Miss E. L. Younghusband, *Ch.* Rep., apps., index. Min. of Health.
1962–63 Cmnd.1973 xxxi		Health and welfare. The development of community care. Plans for the health and welfare services of the local authorities in England & Wales.
1964	Non-Parl.	—— Revision to 1973–74. Min. of Health.
1964	Non-Parl.	Health education. Jt. Cttee. Ld. Cohen of Birkenhead, *Ch.* Rep., apps. Min. of Health.

4. Particular Problems

1959–60 Cmnd.846 viii		Anthrax. Cttee. R. F. Levy, *Ch.* Rep.
1959–60 Cmnd.1105 ix		Human artificial insemination. Dept. Cttee. Ld. Feversham, *Ch.* Rep.
1956	Non-Parl.	Blindness in England, 1951–4. A. Sorsby. Rep., apps. Min. of Health. (See Breviate III, p. 335).
1956	Non-Parl.	Trial case lenses. Cttee. S. Duke-Elder, *Ch.* Rep., app. Min. of Health.
1963	Non-Parl.	Bronchitis. Standing Adv. Cttee. Sub-Cttee. E. G. Oastler, *Ch.* Rep., apps. Scottish Home & Health Dept.
1956	Non-Parl.	Medical care of epileptics. Sub-Cttee. Ld. Cohen of Birkenhead, *Ch.* Rep. Min. of Health.
1961	Non-Parl.	Two-year mass radiography campaign in Scotland, 1957–1958. A study of tuberculosis case-finding by community action. I. M. Macgregor. Rep., apps. Dept. of Health, Scot.
1961	Non-Parl.	Mass miniature radiography. Rep. on three years' examinations in England & Wales, 1955–7. M. A. Heasman. (Studies on Medical and Population Subjects no. 17). General Register Office.
1959	Non-Parl.	Maternity services in Scotland. Cttee. G. L. Montgomery, *Ch.* Rep., apps. Dept. of Health, Scot.
1959	Non-Parl.	Maternity services. Cttee. Ld. Cranbrook, *Ch.* Rep. Min. of Health.
1961	Non-Parl.	Human relations in obstetrics. Standing Adv. Cttee. Rep.

4. Particular Problems—*continued*

1959	Non-Parl.		Standards of normal weight in infancy. Cttee. P. Henderson. Rep. (Reps. on Public Health and Medical Subjects, no. 99). Min. of Health.
1961	Non-Parl.		Prevention of prematurity and the care of premature infants. Jt. Standing Cttees. Sub-Cttee. A. M. Claye, *Ch.* Rep. Min. of Health.
1955–56	Cmd.9623	xxxvi	Law relating to mental illness and mental deficiency in Scotland. Proposals for amendment.
1957	Non-Parl.		Mental deficiency in Scotland. Standing Adv. Cttee. Sub-Cttee. G. M. Fyfe, *Ch.* Rep., app. Dept. of Health, Scot.
1957	Non-Parl.		Welfare needs of mentally handicapped persons. Adv. Council. Cttee. D. K. Fraser, *Ch.* Rep., app. Dept. of Health, Scot.
1956–57	Cmnd.169	xvi	Law relating to mental illness and mental deficiency. R.Com. Ld. Percy of Newcastle, *Ch.* Rep.
1954	Non-Parl.		—— Mins. of ev., 1st–7th days.
1955	Non-Parl.		—— Mins. of ev., 8th–31st days.
1957	Non-Parl.		—— App.
1957	Non-Parl.		—— Index to ev.
1957	Non-Parl.		—— Mins. of ev. taken in private.
1958	Non-Parl.		Mental health legislation. Cttee. J. Dunlop, *Ch.* Rep., app. Dept. of Health, Scot.
1959	Non-Parl.		—— 2nd Rep.
1959–60	Cmnd.931	xxvii	Mental Health (Scotland) Bill. Memo.
1961	Non-Parl.		Mental health services of local health authorities. Standing Adv. Cttee. Mrs. T. M. Allan, *Ch.* Rep. Dept. of Health, Scot.
1961	Non-Parl.		Mental Health (Scotland) Act 1960. Notes on Pt. II. Dept. of Health, Scot.
1962	Non-Parl.		—— Notes on Pts. I & IV. Notes on Pt. V. Scottish Home & Health Dept.
1963	Non-Parl.		—— Notes on Pts. VI & IX. Scottish Home & Health Dept.
1962	Non-Parl.		Training of staff of training centres for the mentally subnormal. Standing Adv. Cttee. Sub-Cttee. J. A. Scott, *Ch.* Rep., apps. Min. of Health.
1962	Non-Parl.		Medical services for child guidance. Standing Adv. Cttee. Sub-Cttee. P. K. McCowan, *Ch.* Rep., apps. Scottish Home & Health Dept.
1957–58	Cmnd.508	vii	Effects of atomic radiation. Statement by the Medical Research Council on the Rep. of the U.N. Scientific Cttee.
1959	Non-Parl.		Radiological hazards to patients. Cttee. Ld. Adrian, *Ch.* Interim Rep., apps. Min. of Health.
1960	Non-Parl.		—— 2nd Rep., apps.
1966	Non-Parl.		—— Final Rep.

4. Particular Problems—*continued*

1955–56 Cmd.9780 xi		Hazards to man of nuclear and allied radiation. Cttee. H. P. Himsworth, *Ch.* Rep.
1960–61 Cmnd.1225 ix		—— 2nd Rep.

1964   Non-Parl.   Exposure of the population to radiation from fallout. Cttee. J. D. Cockcroft, *Ch.* Rep. Medical Research Council.

1964   Non-Parl.   Irradiation of food. Cttee. Working Party. F. G. Young, *Ch.* Rep., apps. Min. of Health.

1957   Non-Parl.   Tobacco smoking and cancer of the lung. Statement. Medical Research Council.

1962   Non-Parl.   Vaccination against smallpox. Memo. rev. ed. Min. of Health.

1963   Non-Parl.   Smallpox 1961–62. (Reps. on Public Health & Medical Subjects no. 109). Min. of Health.

1964   Non-Parl.   Control of outbreaks of smallpox. Memo. Min. of Health.

1957   Non-Parl.   Welfare foods. Standing Adv. Cttees. Jt. Sub-Cttee. Ld. Cohen of Birkenhead, *Ch.* Rep., apps. Min. of Health.

1964   Non-Parl.   Young chronic sick. Sub-Cttee. Ld. Macdonald, *Ch.* Rep., app. Scottish Home & Health Dept.

1962   Non-Parl.   Measures for the control of mosquito nuisances in Great Britain. Memo., apps. rev. ed. Min. of Health.

1961–62 Cmnd.1780 xix   Problem of noise. Cttee. A. H. Wilson, *Ch.* Interim Rep. Noise from motor vehicles.

1962–63 Cmnd.2056 xxii   —— Final Rep.

1956   Non-Parl.   Synthetic detergents. Cttee. H. Jephcott, *Ch.* Rep. Min. of Housing & Local Govt. (See Breviate III, p. 343. See also Synthetic detergents. Standing Technical Cttee. [1st Ann.] Progress Rep.; 1958 Non-Parl. and succeeding Ann. Reps.).

1958   Non-Parl.   Trade effluents. Central Adv. Water Cttee. Sub-Cttee. I. F. Armer, *Ch.* 1st Rep., apps. Min. of Housing & Local Govt.

1960   Non-Parl.   —— Final Rep.

1959   Non-Parl.   Sewage contamination of bathing beaches in England and Wales. Memo. 37. Medical Research Council.

1963   Non-Parl.   Storm overflows and the disposal of storm sewage. Technical Cttee. R. A. Elliott, *Ch.* Interim Rep. Min. of Housing & Local Govt.

5. Drugs and Drug Addiction

1960   Non-Parl.   Drug addiction. Inter-Dept. Cttee. W. R. Brain, *Ch.* Interim Rep. Min. of Health.

1961   Non-Parl.   —— Rep.

1965   Non-Parl.   —— 2nd Rep.

5. Drugs and Drug Addiction—*continued*

1963	Non-Parl.	Safety of drugs. Standing Adv. Cttees. Jt. Sub-Cttee. Ld. Cohen of Birkenhead, *Ch.* Final Rep. Min. of Health. (Interim Rep. not published).
1965	Non-Parl.	Safety of drugs. Cttee. D. Dunlop, *Ch.* [1st] Ann. Rep. Min. of Health. (See succeeding Ann. Reps.).
1964	Non Parl.	Deformities caused by thalidomide. (Reps. on Public Health & Medical Subjects no. 112). Min. of Health.

6. Food Purity

1955–56	Cmd.9757	xvii	Composition and nutritive value of flour. Panel. Ld. Cohen of Birkenhead, *Ch.* Rep.
1958	Non-Parl.		Food poisoning. Memo. Min. of Health.
1961	Non-Parl.		Milk powder. Technical Adv. Cttee. Sub-Cttee. P. K. MacKenzie, *Ch.* Rep. Min. of Agric., Fish. & Food.
1963	Non-Parl.		Antibiotics in milk in Great Britain. Technical Adv. Cttee. Sub-Cttee. A. L. Provan, *Ch.* Rep., app. Min. of Agric., Fish. & Food.
1955–1964			Food standards. Cttee. N. C. Wright, *Ch.* 1955–9; R. Groves, *Ch.* 1960–3; M. W. Perrin, *Ch.* 1964. Reps. Min. of Agric., Fish. & Food. (See Breviate III, p. 345).
1955	Non-Parl.		—— Colouring matters.
1955	Non-Parl.		—— Limits for arsenic in foods. Revised recommendations.
1956	Non-Parl.		—— Processed cheese and cheese spread.
1956	Non'Parl.		—— Limits for copper content of foods.
1956	Non-Parl.		—— Emulsifying and stabilising agents in food.
1956	Non-Parl.		—— Sausages.
1957	Non-Parl.		—— Fluorine content of foods.
1957	Non-Parl.		—— Ice cream standard.
1959	Non-Parl.		—— Soft drinks.
1959	Non-Parl.		—— Preservatives in food. (App. IV contains Rep. of Antibiotics Panel, G. A. Clark, *Ch.*).
1960	Non-Parl.		—— Bread and flour.
1962	Non-Parl.		—— Mineral oil in food.
1962	Non-Parl.		—— Hard, soft and cream cheeses.
1962	Non-Parl.		—— Canned meat.
1962	Non-Parl.		—— Dried milk.
1963	Non-Parl.		—— Meat pies.
1963	Non-Parl.		—— Antioxidants in food.
1964	Non-Parl.		—— Colouring matters.
1964	Non-Parl.		—— Food labelling.

XII. HOUSING AND TOWN AND COUNTRY PLANNING

1. Housing

1955–56	Cmd.9559	xxi	Ministry of Housing & Local Government. Rep. for period 1950/51 to 1954. (For succeeding Ann. Reps. see p. 99).

1. Housing—*continued*

1955–56	Cmd.9593	xxxvi	Slum clearance (England & Wales). Summary of returns including proposals submitted by local authorities under Sect. 1 of the Housing Repairs and Rents Act, 1954.
1955–56	Cmd.9685	xxxvi	Slum clearance. Summary of proposals by local authorities for dealing with unfit houses under the Housing (Repairs and Rents) (Scotland) Act, 1954.
1956–57	Cmnd.17	xxvi	Rent control. Statistical information.
1956	Non-Parl.		Housing subsidies in Scotland. Working Party. J. C. Wilson, *Ch.* Rep., apps. Dept. of Health, Scot.
1958	Non-Parl.		Rents of corporation houses in Glasgow. Inquiry. C. J. D. Shaw. Rep. Dept. of Health, Scot.
1960–61	Cmnd.1246	xx	Rent Act, 1957. Inquiry. P. G. Gray, E. Parr. Rep.
1961	Non-Parl.		Review of rents of council houses in Dunbarton. Local Inquiry. G. C. Emslie. Rep. Dept. of Health, Scot.
1963	Non-Parl.		Rents of corporation houses in Dundee. Inquiry. M. Kissen. Rep., app. Scottish Development Dept.
1958–59	Cmnd.571	xxv	House purchase. Proposed government scheme.
1959–60	Cmnd.872	ix	Caravans as homes. A. Wilson. Rep.
1962	Non-Parl.		Caravan parks. Location, layout, landscape. Min. of Housing & Local Govt.
1960–61	Cmnd.1290	xxvii	Housing in England & Wales [Role of private enterprise, public authorities, etc.]. Proposals.
1961–62	Cmnd.1520	xxx	Housing in Scotland. Statement.
1962–63	Cmnd.2050	xxx	Housing [government proposals for expanding the provision of houses].
1963	Non-Parl.		U.K. housing mission to Canada. Rep., app. Min. of Public Building & Works.
			Central Housing Adv. Cttee. Housing Management Sub-Cttee. Min. of Housing & Local Govt. (See Breviate III, pp. 360–3).
1955	Non-Parl.		—— 5th Rep. Residential qualifications. P. L. Leigh-Breese, *Ch.*
1955	Non-Parl.		—— 6th Rep. Unsatisfactory tenants. P. L. Leigh-Breese, *Ch.*
1956	Non-Parl.		—— Rep. Moving from the slums. J. M. Mackintosh, *Ch.*
1959	Non-Parl.		—— Rep. Councils and their houses. Lady Reading, *Ch.*
1961	Non-Parl.		—— Rep. Homes for today and tomorrow. P. Morris, *Ch.*
1964	Non-Parl.		Costing of management and maintenance of local authority housing. Working Party. F. J. Ward, *Ch.* Rep., apps. Min. of Housing & Local Govt.

1. Housing—*continued*

1962–63 Cmnd.1952 xxxi   London: employment, housing, land.

1958   Non-Parl.   Services of Valuation Office, Inland Revenue. Availability to local authorities in Scotland. Memo. Dept. of Health, Scot.

1958   Non-Parl.   Causes of damage to houses at Hatfield new town. Inquiry. M. E. Rowe. Rep. Min. of Housing & Local Govt.

2. Town and Country Planning

The policies and techniques of town and country planning also play an important part in regional planning. Papers on Regional Development will be found on pp. 43–4.

1955   Non-Parl.   Town and Country Planning Acts, 1947 & 1954. Revised system of exchequer grants to local authorities. Memo., apps. Min. of Housing & Local Govt.

1955   Non-Parl.   Town and Country Planning (Scotland) Acts, 1947 & 1954. Revised scheme of exchequer grants to local planning authorities. Memo., apps. Dept. of Health, Scot.

1958–59 Cmnd.562 xxv   Town and Country Planning Bill. Memo.

1961–62 Cmnd.1787 xxiv   Position of 'third parties' at planning appeal inquiries. Council on Tribunals. Ld. Tenby, *Ch.* Rep.

1955   Non-Parl.   Draft New Town (Cumbernauld) Designation Order, 1955. Memo., apps. Dept. of Health, Scot.

1958   Non-Parl.   Proposed development of land at Lymm for Manchester overspill. Inquiry. J. R. Willis, *Ch.* Rep., apps. Min. of Housing & Local Govt.

1961   Non-Parl.   Draft of the Skelmersdale New Town (Designation) Order, 1961. Inquiry. A. R. Manktelow, *Ch.* Rep. Min. of Housing & Local Govt.

1962   Non-Parl.   Draft New Town (Livingston) Designation Order, 1962. Memo., apps. Dept. of Health, Scot.

1962–63 (281)   xxii   Commission for the New Towns. [1st Ann.] Rep. (see succeeding Ann. Reps.).

1962   Non-Parl.   Green belts. Min. of Housing & Local Govt.

1962   Non-Parl.   Caravan parks. Location, layout, landscape. Min. of Housing & Local Govt.

1960   Non-Parl.   Control of mineral working. Memo., app., index. rev. ed. Min. of Housing & Local Govt.

1963   Non-Parl.   Town and Country Planning Act, 1962. Town and Country Planning (National Coal Board) Regulations, 1963. Memo. Min. of Housing & Local Govt.

3. Smoke Control

Clean Air Act, 1956. Memos. Min. of Housing & Local Govt. Dept. of Health, Scot.

1956   Non-Parl.   —— Smoke control areas.

3. Smoke Control—*continued*

1956	Non-Parl.	—— Miscellaneous provisions.
1958	Non-Parl.	—— Industrial provisions.
1959–60 Cmnd.999	ix	Solid smokeless fuels. Cttee. N. M. Peech, *Ch.* Rep.
1959–60 Cmnd.1113	xxvii	Smoke control (England & Wales). Summary of programmes submitted by local authorities for the establishment of smoke control areas.
1962–63 Cmnd.1890	xxxi	Smoke control (England & Wales), 1962–66. Summary of programmes submitted by local authorities.
1963–64 Cmnd.2231	xxvi	Domestic fuel supplies and the clean air policy.

XIV. EDUCATION

1. General Policy, Schools

1956	Non-Parl.	Closure of schools and exclusion from school on account of infectious illness. Memo., apps. Min. of Educ., etc.
1957	Non-Parl.	Educational maintenance allowances. [Grants for secondary education, extended year.] Working Party. T. R. Weaver, *Ch.* Rep., apps. Min. of Educ.
1958–59 Cmnd.603	xxv	Education in Scotland: the next step.
1958–59 Cmnd.604	xxv	Secondary education for all. A new drive.
1959	Non-Parl.	15 to 18. Central Adv. Council, England. G. Crowther, *Ch.* Vol. 1. Rep., apps., index. Min. of Educ.
1960	Non-Parl.	—— Vol. II. Surveys, index.
1961–62 Cmnd.1538	xiii	Transfer from primary to secondary education. Adv. Council, Scotland. Special Cttee. T. M. Knox, *Ch.* Rep.
1962	Non-Parl.	Forward from school. The links between school and further education. Enquiry. Rep. Min. of Educ.
1963	Non-Parl.	From school to further education. Working Party. J. S. Brunton, *Ch.* Rep., apps. Scottish Educ. Dept.
1963	Non-Parl.	Half our future. Central Adv. Council, England. J. H. Newsom, *Ch.* Rep., apps., index. Min. of Educ.
1956	Non-Parl.	Working of the school meals service. Inquiry. Rep., apps. Min. of Educ.
1960	Non-Parl.	Education in rural Wales. Central Adv. Council, Wales. A. B. Oldfield-Davies, *Ch.* Rep., apps. Min. of Educ.
1960	Non-Parl.	Assistance with the cost of boarding education. [To consider the needs of pupils whose parents are overseas . . . what is the criteria used by the L.E.A. for determining needs.] Working Party. L. C. J. Martin, *Ch.* Rep., apps. Min. of Educ.

2. Particular Problems and Further Education

i. Handicapped Children, Curriculum, Examinations, Crafts, Language

1955	Non-Parl.	Maladjusted children. Cttee. J. E. A. Underwood, *Ch.* Rep., apps., index. Min. of Educ.
1961	Non-Parl.	Degrees of mental handicap. Standards of ascertainment for Scottish schoolchildren. Working Party. N. D. Walker, *Ch.* Rep., app. Scottish Educ. Dept.
1963	Non-Parl.	Survey of deaf children who have been transferred from special schools or units to ordinary schools. E. M. Johnson (Miss). Rep., app. Min. of Educ.
1959	Non-Parl.	Curriculum of the senior secondary school. Introduction of the ordinary grade of the Scottish Leaving Certificate. Working Party. J. S. Brunton, *Ch.* Rep., app. Scottish Educ. Dept.
1959–60 Cmnd.1068 xii		The post-fourth year examination structure in Scotland. Adv. Council, Scotland. Special Cttee. T. M. Knox, *Ch.* Rep.
		Secondary School Examinations Council. J. F. Lockwood, *Ch.* Min. of Educ. (See Breviate III, p. 402.)
1960	Non-Parl.	—— Secondary school examinations other than the G.C.E. Cttee. R. Beloe, *Ch.* Rep., apps.
1960	Non-Parl.	—— 3rd Rep., apps. General Certificate of Education and Sixth form studies.
1961	Non-Parl.	—— 4th Rep., apps. Certificate of secondary education. Proposal for a new school leaving certificate other than the G.C.E.
1962	Non-Parl.	—— 5th Rep. Certificate of secondary education. Notes for the guidance of regional examining bodies.
1962	Non-Parl.	—— 6th Rep., apps. Sixth form studies and university entrance requirements.
1963	Non-Parl.	—— 7th Rep., apps. Scope and standards of the certificate of secondary education.
1964	Non-Parl.	—— 8th Rep., apps. The examining of English language.
1964	Non-Parl.	Schools curricula and examinations. Working Party. J. F. Lockwood, *Ch.* Rep., apps. Dept. of Educ. & Science.
1956	Non-Parl.	The Arts in Education. Art and Crafts in the schools of Wales. Central Adv. Council, Wales. A. B. Oldfield-Davies, *Ch.* Rep., apps. Min. of Educ. (See Breviate III, p. 406.)
1962	Non-Parl.	Teaching of Russian. Cttee. N. G. Annan, *Ch.* Rep., apps. Min. of Educ., etc.
1963–64 Cmnd.2198 xx		Welsh language today. Council for Wales & Monmouthshire. R. I. Aaron, *Ch.* Rep.

ii. Further Education

1957	Non-Parl.	Proposed changes in the art examinations and in the length of the diploma course. Nat. Adv. Cttee. F. L. Freeman, *Ch.* Rep. Min. of Educ.

2. Particular Problems and Further Education—*continued*

1960	Non-Parl.	Art education. Nat. Adv. Council. W. M. Coldstream, *Ch.* 1st Rep., app. Min. of Educ.
1962	Non-Parl.	—— 2nd Rep., apps. Vocational courses in colleges and schools of art. W. M. Coldstream, *Ch.* Min. of Educ.
1964	Non-Parl.	—— 3rd Rep., app. Post-diploma studies in art and design. W. M. Coldstream. *Ch.* Dept. of Educ. & Science.
1957	Non-Parl.	Agriculture and dairy diploma courses in Wales. Cttee. D. S. Davies, *Ch.* Rep., apps. Min. of Agric., Fish. & Food.
1958	Cmnd.614 xi	Further education for agriculture provided by local education authorities. Cttee. Ld. De la Warr, *Ch.* Rep.
1960	Non-Parl.	Welsh agricultural college. Working Party. J. M. Jones, *Ch.* Rep. Min. of Agric., Fish. & Food.

iii. Technical Education

1955–56	Cmd.9703 xxxvi	Technical education.
1958	Non-Parl.	Provision of advanced technical education at the technical colleges at Wrexham, Denbighshire and Kelsterton, Flintshire. Adv. Panel. W. H. S. Chance, *Ch.* Rep., app. Min. of Educ.
1961	Non-Parl.	Technical education in Wales. Central Adv. Council, Wales. A. B. Oldfield-Davies, *Ch.* Rep., apps. Min. of Educ.
1960–61	Cmnd.1245 xxvii	Technical education in Scotland. Pattern for the future.
1960–61	Cmnd.1254 xxvii	Better opportunities in technical education.
1962	Non-Parl.	General studies in technical colleges. Cttee. C. R. English, *Ch.* Rep. Min. of Educ.
1964	Non-Parl.	Day release. [Release from work for technical education.] Cttee. C. Henniker-Heaton, *Ch.* Rep., apps. Dept. of Educ. & Science.
1959	Non-Parl.	Further education for commerce. National Adv. Council. Adv. Cttee. J. G. McMeeking, *Ch.* Rep., apps. Min. of Educ.
1962	Non-Parl.	Management studies in technical colleges. Adv. Council. J. W. Platt, *Ch.* 1st Rep., apps. Min. of Educ.
1964	Non-Parl.	A higher award in business studies. Nat. Adv. Council. Adv. Sub-Cttee. W. F. Crick, *Ch.* Rep., app. Dept. of Educ. & Science.

3. Teachers, Youth Leaders: Training, Supply, Salaries

1955	Non-Parl.	Grants to training college students. Working Party. A. E. M. Davies, *Ch.* Rep., apps. Min. of Educ.
1956–1962		Training and supply of teachers. Nat. Adv. Council. Min. of Educ. (See Breviate III, p. 420.)

3. Teachers, Youth Leaders: Training, Supply, Salaries—*continued*

1956	Non-Parl.	—— 5th Rep. Three year training for teachers. P. R. Morris, *Ch.*
1957	Non-Parl.	—— 6th Rep. Scope and content of the three year course of teacher training. P. R. Morris, *Ch.*
1962	Non-Parl.	—— 7th Rep., apps. Demand and supply of teachers, 1960–80. J. S. Fulton, *Ch.*
1962	Non-Parl.	—— 8th Rep., app. Future pattern of the education and training of teachers. J. S. Fulton, *Ch.*
1958	Non-Parl.	Supply of teachers in the 1960s. Correspondence. Min. of Educ.
1958	Non-Parl.	Future demand for teachers. Correspondence. Min. of Educ.
1957	Non-Parl.	Supply and training of teachers for technical colleges. Special Cttee. W. Jackson, *Ch.* Rep., apps. Min. of Educ.
1961	Non-Parl.	Teachers for further education. Nat. Adv. Council. Sub-Cttee. E. L. Russell, *Ch.* Rep., apps. Min. of Educ.
1963	Non-Parl.	Women and teaching. Nuffield Survey. R. K. Kelsall. Rep. Min. of Educ.
1959–60 Cmnd.929 xxi		Youth service in England and Wales. [To review the contribution . . . and to advise according to what priorities best value can be obtained for the money spent.] Cttee. Lady Albemarle, *Ch.* Rep., apps.
1962	Non-Parl.	Training of part-time youth leaders and assistants. Working Party. G. S. Bessey, *Ch.* Rep. Min. of Educ.
1954–55 Cmd.9419 iv		Supply of teachers of mathematics and science in Scotland. Cttee. E. V. Appleton, *Ch.* Rep.
1956	Non-Parl.	Qualifications of teachers in schools holding the teacher's technical certificate. Cttee. H. H. Donnelly, *Ch.* Rep., apps. Scottish Educ. Dept.
1956–57 Cmnd.196 x		Supply of teachers in Scotland. Dept. Cttee. T. G. Stewart, *Ch.* 3rd Rep. (See Breviate III, p. 419.)
1961–62 Cmnd.1601 xiii		—— 4th Rep. A. G. Rodger, *Ch.*
1956–57 Cmnd.202 x		Measures to improve the supply of teachers in Scotland. Adv. Council, Scotland. Special Cttee. T. M. Knox, *Ch.* Interim Rep.
1958–59 Cmnd.644 xi		—— Rep.
1962	Non-Parl.	Appointment of teachers to education committees. Working Party. H. H. Donnelly, *Ch.* Rep. Scottish Educ. Dept.
1962	Non-Parl.	Relations between education authorities and teachers. Working Party. B. J. F. Stewart, *Ch.* Rep., apps. Scottish Educ. Dept.
1962–63 Cmnd.2066 xv		The teaching profession in Scotland. Arrangements for the award and withdrawal of certificates of competency to teach. Cttee. Ld. Wheatley, *Ch.* Rep.

3. Teachers, Youth Leaders: Training, Supply, Salaries—*continued*

1962	Non-Parl.		Consultation on educational matters between the Teachers' Associations and the Scottish Education Department. Working Party. J. Craigie, *Ch.* Rep., apps. Scottish Educ. Dept.
1954–55	Cmd.9365	iv	Structure of further education salaries. Working Party. T. G. Stewart, *Ch.* Rep.
			Scales of salaries for teachers. Burnham Cttee. Ld. McNair, *Ch.* Reps. Min. of Educ. (See Breviate III, p. 421).
1956	Non-Parl.		—— Further education.
1956	Non-Parl.		—— Primary and secondary schools.
1956	Non-Parl.		—— Training colleges.
1956	Non-Parl.		—— Farm institutes, etc.
1959	Non-Parl.		Scales of salaries for teachers. Burnham Cttee. T. P. Creed, *Ch.* 4 Reps.
1961–1962	Non-Parl.		Scales of salaries for teachers. Burnham Cttee. T. P. Creed, *Ch.* 4 Reps.
1963	Non-Parl.		Scales of salaries for teachers. Burnham Cttee. 4 Reps. reprinted as amended 1963.
1960–61	(269)	xxi	Teachers (Superannuation) Acts 1918–1956. Government Actuary. Rep.
1961–62	(311)	xxiv	Teachers Superannuation Act, 1925. Government Actuary, Rep. on the 1926 scheme.
1959	Non-Parl.		Basis of remuneration of part-time further education teachers. Working Party. H. H. Donnelly, *Ch.* Rep., apps. Scottish Educ. Dept.
1956	Non-Parl.		Draft superannuation scheme for teachers (Scotland) 1956. Scottish Educ. Dept.
1957–58	Cmnd.527	x	Pensions for the widows, children and dependants of teachers in Scotland. Working Party. T. G. Stewart, *Ch.* Rep.
1961–62	(100)	xxiv	Teachers superannuation scheme (Scotland) 1948–1956. Government Actuary. Rep.
1962	Non-Parl.		Pensions for teachers' widows. Working Party. H. H. Donnelly, *Ch.* Rep., apps. Scottish Educ. Dept.

4. Universities and Higher Commonwealth Education

i. Universities

1956–57	Cmnd.9	xix	Methods used by universities of contracting and of recording and controlling expenditure. U.G.C. Sub-Cttee. G. H. Gater, *Ch.* Rep.
1960–61	Cmnd.1235	xxi	Methods used by universities of contracting and of recording and controlling expenditure. Review of the application by universities of the procedures recommended by Sir George Gater's Cttee. A. N. Rucker.
1957	Non-Parl.		Halls of residence. U.G.C. Sub-Cttee. W. R. Niblett, *Ch.* Rep., apps. Treasury.

4. Universities and Higher Commonwealth Education—*continued*

1958–59 Cmnd.640 xix	Local contributions to the Scottish universities. Special Cttee. Ld. Sorn (J. G. McIntyre), *Ch.* Rep.
1959–60 Cmnd.1051 xxi	Grants to students. Cttee. C. K. Anderson, *Ch.* Rep.
1961 Non-Parl.	Oriental, Slavonic, East European and African studies. U.G.C. Sub-Cttee. W. G. Hayter, *Ch.* Rep., app. Treasury.
1962 Non-Parl.	Postgraduate medical education and the specialties. With special reference to the problem in London. U.G.C. Cttee. G. W. Pickering, *Ch.* Rep. (Reps. on Public Health & Medical Subjects, 106). Min. of Health.
1963 Non-Parl.	University teaching methods. U.G.C. Cttee. E. Hale, *Ch.* Interim Rep., Use of vacations by students, apps. Treasury.
1964 Non-Parl.	—— Rep., apps. Dept. of Educ. & Science.
1962–63 Cmnd.2154 xi –II–I Cmnd.2154	Higher education. Cttee. Ld. Robbins, *Ch.* Rep., index.
–I xi Cmnd.2154	—— App. 1. Demand for places in higher education.
–II xii Cmnd.2154	—— App. 2(A). Students and their education.
–II–I xii Cmnd.2154	—— App. 2(B). Students and their education.
–III xii Cmnd.2154	—— App. 3. Teachers in higher education.
–IV xii	—— App. 4. Administrative, financial and economic aspects of higher education.
Cmnd.2154 –V xiii Cmnd.2154	—— App. 5. Higher education in other countries.
–VI to VIII xiii	—— Evidence Pt. I, Written and oral evidence, Vols. A–C.
Cmnd.2154 –IX to XI xiv	—— Evidence Pt. I, Written and oral evidence, Vols. D–F.
Cmnd.2154 –XII xiv	—— Evidence Pt. II, Documentary evidence.
1963–64 Cmnd.2165 xxvi	Higher education. Government statement.
1963–64 Cmnd.2419 viii	Demand for agricultural graduates. Inter-Dept. Cttee C.I.C. Bosanquet, *Ch.* Rep.
1962 Non-Parl.	D.S.I.R., universities and colleges, 1956–60. Rep., apps. D.S.I.R.
1963 Non-Parl.	First employment of university graduates, 1961–62. U.G.C. Treasury (See succeeding annual publications).
1964 Non-Parl.	University Appointments Boards. U.G.C. Ld. Heyworth. Rep., apps. Dept. of Educ. & Science.

4. Universities and Higher Commonwealth Education—*continued*

1956–57 Cmnd.79 xix	University development, 1952–56. U.G.C. K. A. H. Murray, *Ch*. Interim Rep.
1957–58 Cmnd.534 xviii	—— Rep. 1952–57.
1961–62 Cmnd.1691 xxiv	University development, 1957–61. U.G.C. K. A. H. Murray, *Ch*. Interim Rep.
1963–64 Cmnd.2267 xx	—— Rep. 1957–1962.
1960 Non-Parl.	Superannuation of university teachers. U.G.C. Cttee. E. Hale, *Ch*. Rep., apps. Treasury.
1963–64 Cmnd.2317 xvii	Remuneration of academic staff in universities and colleges of advanced technology. Nat. Incomes Com. F. G. Lawrence, *Ch*. Rep.

ii. Higher Education in Commonwealth Countries

See Annex 1. Commonwealth Countries, p. 91.

5. Libraries, Art Galleries, Museums

i. Libraries, Public Records

1960 Non-Parl.	Work of the Public Record Office. Keeper of Public Records. 1st Ann. Rep. and 1st Rep. of the Adv. Council. Ld. Chancellor's Office. (See succeeding Ann. Reps.).
1958–59 Cmnd. 660 xvi	Structure of the public library service in England and Wales. Cttee. S. C. Roberts, *Ch*. Rep.
1962 Non-Parl.	Standards of public library service in England and Wales. Working Party. H. T. Bourdillon, *Ch*. Rep., apps. Min. of Educ.
1962 Non-Parl.	Inter-library co-operation in England and Wales. Working Party. E. B. H. Baker, *Ch*. Rep., apps.

ii. Art Galleries, Museums

1955 Non-Parl.	Works of art in the House of Commons. Adv. Cttee. Ld. Hinchingbrooke, *Ch*. Rep., apps. Min. of Works.
1955–56 Cmd.9595 xvii	Export of works of art. Reviewing Cttee. 2nd Rep. (See Breviate III, p. 433, also succeeding Ann. Reps.).
1958 Non-Parl.	Government and the arts in Britain. Rep., apps. Treasury.
1959–60 Cmnd.982 xiv	Royal Fine Art Com. for Scotland. H. Hetherington, *Ch*. 1st Rep., 1927–1959. (See succeeding Reps., published irregularly).
1959, 1961	Housing the arts in Great Britain. Arts Council. Cttees. W. Griffith, R. Kemp, R. E. Presswood, *Chs*. Reps., Pt. I, London, Scotland, Wales. Pt. II, Needs of the English provinces (not published by H.M.S.O.).

5. Libraries, Art Galleries, Museums—*continued*

1959	Non-Parl.	Museums and galleries. Standing Com. 5th Rep., 1954–1958, apps. Standing Com. (See Breviate III, p. 430, and succeeding Reps. published irregularly).
1961–62	Cmnd.1750 xviii	Security at the National Gallery. Ld. Bridges, J. F. Ferguson. Abridged Rep.
1964	Non-Parl.	Sale of works of art by public bodies. Cttee. Ld. Cottesloe, *Ch.* Rep., apps. Treasury.

6. Scientific and Social Research

For further items on research see Government Departments, p. 28–9 and Research and Development, p. 47.

1956	Non-Parl.	Social and economic research. Inter-Dept. Cttee. G. North, *Ch.* Rep. Ld. President's Office.
1962	Non-Parl.	Oceanographic and meteorological research in relation to sea defence. Adv. Cttee. J. Proudman, *Ch.* 1st Rep. [Floods]. Min. of Agric., Fish. & Food.
1962–63	Cmnd.2029 xxiv	Effects of high altitude nuclear explosions on scientific experiments. Working Party. J. A. Ratcliffe, *Ch.* Rep.

XV. SOCIAL PROBLEMS

1. Child Care

1955	Non-Parl.	Boarding-out of children regulations 1955. Memo. Home Office.
1956	Non-Parl.	Care of children under five years of age. Memo. Home Office.
1959	Non-Parl.	Children's homes. Memo., app. Scottish Home Dept.
1959	Non-Parl.	Boarding-out of children. Memo., app. Scottish Home Dept.
1964	Non-Parl.	Needs of young children in care. Memo. Home Office.
1959–60	Cmnd.1191 ix	Children and young persons. Dept. Cttee. Ld. Ingleby, *Ch.* Rep., apps.
1963–64	Cmnd.2306 ix	Children and young persons, Scotland. Cttee. Ld. Kilbrandon, Rep.
1962–63	Cmnd.1966 ix	Prevention of neglect of children. Adv. Council. Cttee. J. McBoyle, *Ch.* Rep.
1963	Non-Parl.	Staffing of local authority Children's Departments Scottish Adv. Council. Lady Elliot, *Ch.* Rep., apps. Scottish Home & Health Dept.
1963	Non-Parl.	Child care service at work. T. Burns, S. Sinclair. Rep. Scottish Educ. Dept.
1958–59	Cmnd.842 xvi	Conflicts of jurisdiction affecting children. Cttee. F. L. C. Hodson, *Ch.* Rep.

2. Charities

1955–56 Cmd.9538 xxxvi   Charitable trusts in England and Wales. Government Policy. (See Breviate III, pp. 447–9).

1958–59 Cmnd.831 xix   Rating of charities and kindred bodies. Cttee. F. E. Pritchard, *Ch.* Rep.

3. Betting

1959–60 Cmnd.1003 xvi   Levy on betting on horse races. Dept. Cttee. L. E. Peppiatt, *Ch.* Rep.

1963–64 Cmnd.2275 xiii   Gaming. Customs & Excise Com. Enquiry. Rep.

4. Licensing

1956–57 Cmnd.168 xv   Allegations made by the Civil Service Union relating to Carlisle & District Management Scheme. Enquiry. C. S. S. Burt, *Ch.* Rep.

1960–61 Cmnd.1217 xviii   Scottish licensing law. Cttee. C. W. G. Guest, *Ch.* 1st Rep.

1962–63 Cmnd.2021 xx   —— 2nd Rep.

XVI. LEGAL ADMINISTRATION

1. Legal Administration, Procedure, Legal Aid

1955–56 Cmd.9524 xxiii   Summary trial of minor offences. Dept. Cttee. R. T. Sharpe, *Ch.* Rep.

1957–58 Cmnd.479 xv   Proceedings before examining justices. Dept. Cttee. Ld. Tucker, *Ch.* Rep.

1958–59 Cmnd.818 xiii   Funds in Court. Cttee. C. H. Pearson, *Ch.* Rep.

1958–59 Cmnd.842 xvi   Conflicts of jurisdiction affecting children. Cttee. F. L. C. Hodson, *Ch.* Rep.

1959–60 Cmnd.967 xvii   Chancery Chambers and the Chancery Registrar's Office. Cttee. Ld. Harman, *Ch.* Rep.

1960–61 Cmnd.1289 xiii   Business of the criminal courts. Inter-Dept. Cttee. G. H. B. Streatfeild, *Ch.* Rep.

1961–62 Cmnd.1606 xviii   Magistrates' courts in London. Inter-Dept. Cttee. C. D. Aarvold, *Ch.* Rep.

1961–62 Cmnd.1616 xii   Commercial court users' Conference. C. Miller, *Ch.* Rep.

1956–57 Cmnd.227 xix   Supreme Court of Northern Ireland. Cttee. C. L. Sheil, *Ch.* Rep.

1957–58 Cmnd.456 xv   Diligence. Cttee. H. Mckechnie, *Ch.* Rep.

1959–60 Cmnd.851 xvii   Civil jury trials in Scotland. Cttee. J. F. Strachan, *Ch.* Rep.

1961 Non-Parl.   Expenses of legal proceedings against justices and clerks. Working Party. W. T. C. Skyrme, *Ch.* Rep., app. Home Office, etc.

1. Legal Administration, Procedure, Legal Aid—*continued*

1959–60 Cmnd.918 xvii	Financial provisions of the Legal Aid and Advice Act, 1949, and the Legal Aid (Assessment of Resources) Regulations, 1950. Adv. Cttee. Ld. Bridgeman, *Ch.* Rep.
1959–60 Cmnd.1015 xvii	Legal aid in criminal proceedings. Cttee. Ld. Guthrie, *Ch.* Rep.
1959–60 Cmnd.962 xvii	Proviso to Sect. 2(1) of the Legal Aid and Advice Act, 1949. Adv. Cttee. Ld. Bridgeman, *Ch.* Rep.
1962 Non-Parl.	Legal aid in criminal proceedings. Working Party. R. R. Pittam, *Ch.* 1st Rep., apps. Home Office, etc.
1963 Non-Parl.	—— Final Rep., apps.
1960–61 Cmnd.1406 xiii	Compensation for victims of crimes of violence.
1961–62 Cmnd.1829 xx	Limitation of actions in cases of personal injury. Cttee. E. Davies, *Ch.* Rep.
1963–64 Cmnd.2323 xxvi	Compensation for victims of crimes of violence.

2. Police

1955–56 (114–I) ix	Police (Scot.) Bill [H.L.] Jt. Sel. Cttee. Ld. Balfour of Burleigh, *Ch.* Rep., proc., mins. of ev.
1956–57 Cmnd.251 xviii	Administration and efficiency of Cardiganshire Constabulary and state of discipline in the force. Inquiry. Rep.
1957–58 Cmnd.374 xvii	Proposed compulsory amalgamation of Police Forces of County of Carmarthen and County of Cardigan. Inquiry. H. I. Nelson, *Ch.* Rep.
1958 Non-Parl.	Police uniform. Police Council. Cttee. W. J. A. Willis, *Ch.* Rep., apps. Home Office.
1958 Non-Parl.	Police pensions regulations. Commutation and allocation. Explanatory Memo. Home Office, etc.
1960–61 Cmnd.1222 xx	Police. R. Com. H. Willink, *Ch.* Interim Rep.
1961–62 Cmnd.1728 xx	—— Final Rep.
1960 Non-Parl.	—— Mins. of ev., 1st–10th days.
1960 Non-Parl.	—— App. to mins. of ev. (1–10).
1961 Non-Parl.	—— Mins. of ev., 11th–27th days.
1962 Non-Parl.	—— Apps. II–IV.
1963 Non-Parl.	—— Index to ev. and apps.
1960–61 Cmnd.1450 xxvii	Police training in England and Wales.
1962 Non-Parl.	Higher police training. Police Council. Cttee. K. A. L. Parker, *Ch.* Rep., app. Home Office.
1963 Non-Parl.	—— 2nd Rep. Senior staff course.
1963 Non-Parl.	—— Supplementary Rep. Special course at the Police College.
1963–64 Cmnd.2176 xviii	Sheffield police appeal. Inquiry. G. R. Swanwick, *Ch.* Rep.
1963–64 Cmnd.2319 xviii	Action of the Metropolitan Police in relation to the case of Mr. Herman Woolf. Inquiry. N. J. Skelhorn. Rep.

3. Prisons, Penal System, Treatment of Offenders, Probation and After-care

1957–58 Cmnd.544 xvii — Remuneration and conditions of service of certain grades in the prison service. Cttee. H. Wynn Parry, *Ch*. Rep.

1958–59 Cmnd.645 xxv — Penal practice in a changing society. Aspects of future development (England and Wales).

1963–64 Cmnd.2296 xxv — War against crime in England and Wales, 1959–1964.

1964 Non-Parl. — Sentence of the court. A handbook for courts on the treatment of offenders. Home Office.

1957 Non-Parl. — Alternatives to short terms of imprisonment. Adv. Council. Ld. Drogheda, *Ch*. H. Studdy, *Ch*. of Sub-Cttee. Rep., apps. (App. D, Rep. of Adv. Council on the suspended sentence, 1952). Home Office.

1960 Non-Parl. — Use of short sentences of imprisonment by the courts. Scottish Adv. Council. Cttee. A. B. Hume, *Ch*, Rep., apps. Scottish Home Dept.

1959 Non-Parl. — Treatment of young offenders. Adv. Council. P. R. Barry. *Ch*. Rep. Home Office.

1959–60 Cmnd.1191 ix — Children and young persons. Dept. Cttee. Ld. Ingleby, *Ch*. Rep., apps.

1963–64 Cmnd.2306 ix — Children and young persons, Scotland. Cttee. Ld. Kilbrandon, *Ch*. Rep.

1960 Non-Parl. — Custodial sentences for young offenders. Scottish Adv. Council. H. R. Leslie, *Ch*. Rep., app. Scottish Home Dept.

1962 Non-Parl. — Custodial training for young offenders. Scottish Adv. Council. Cttee. W. J. Bryden, *Ch*. Rep., apps. Scottish Home & Health Dept.

1962 Non-Parl. — Non-residential treatment of offenders under 21. Adv. Council. P. R. Barry, *Ch*. Rep., apps. Home Office.

1962 Non-Parl. — Medical services for child guidance [Psychiatric services for purposes of the Criminal Justice Act, 1949], Standing Adv. Cttee. Sub-Cttee. P. K. Mc-Cowan, *Ch*. Rep., apps. Scottish Home & Health Dept.

1963 Non-Parl. — Preventive detention. Adv. Council. Sub-Cttee. R. C. Mortimer, *Ch*. Rep., apps. Home Office.

1961 Non-Parl. — Work for prisoners. Adv. Council. G. W. Anson, *Ch*. Rep. Home Office.

1964 Non-Parl. — Organisation of work for prisoners. Adv. Council. G. W. Anson, *Ch*. Rep. Home Office.

1963 Non-Parl. — Work and vocational training in Borstals. Adv. Council. G. W. Anson, *Ch*. Rep. Home Office.

1957–58 Cmnd.503 xvii — Allegations of ill-treatment of prisoners in H.M. Prison, Liverpool. Inquiry. G. R. Vick, *Ch*. Rep.

3. Prisons, Penal System, Treatment of Offenders, Probation and After-care—*continued*

1958–59	Cmnd.718 xvi	Allegation of assault on John Waters. Tribunal. Ld. Sorn, *Ch.* Rep.
1959	Non-Parl.	—— Proceedings. Scottish Home Dept.
1962–63	Cmnd.2068 xxiii	Allegations of ill-treatment of prisoners in H.M. Prison, Durham. Inquiry. T. R. Percy, *Ch.* Rep.
1959–60	Cmnd.937 ix	Disturbance at the Carlton approved school on Aug. 29 and 30, 1959. Inquiry. V. Durand. Rep.
1961–62	Cmnd.1588 xxiii	Remand homes. Scottish Adv. Council. Special Cttee. R. W. B. Ellis, *Ch.* Rep.
1960–61	Cmnd.1213 xiii	Corporal punishment. Adv. Council. P. R. Barry, *Ch.* Rep.
1954	Non-Parl.	Central After-Care Association. Ann. Rep. Home Office. (See succeeding Ann. Reps.).
1958	Non-Parl.	After-care and supervision of discharged prisoners. Adv. Council. Sub-Cttee. B. J. Hartwell, *Ch:* Rep., apps. Home Office.
1963	Non-Parl.	Organisation of after-care. Adv. Council. Sub-Cttee. B. J. Hartwell, *Ch.* Rep., apps. Home Office.
1961	Non-Parl.	Extension of compulsory after-care to additional categories of inmates and prisoners. Scottish Adv. Council. H. R. Leslie, *Ch.* Rep. Scottish Home Dept.
1961–62	Cmnd.1650 xxiii	Probation service. Dept. Cttee. R. P. Morison, *Ch.* Rep.
1961–62	Cmnd.1800 xxiii	—— 2nd Rep.
1961	Non-Parl.	Probation Service in Scotland. 3rd edition. Scottish Home Dept.
1964	Non-Parl.	Organisation of the prison medical service. Working Party. E. H. Gwynn, *Ch.* Rep., apps.

4. Law of Property

1955–56	Cmd.9825 xxii	Land charges. Cttee. R. F. Roxburgh, *Ch.* Rep.
1957–58	Cmnd.473 xvii	Law relating to rights of light. Cttee. C. E. Harman, *Ch.* Rep.
1961–62	Cmnd.1789 xviii	Residential leasehold property. Summary of reports by professional bodies.
1957–58	Cmnd.472 xviii	Tenancy of Shops (Scotland) Act, 1949. Cttee. A. Shearer, *Ch.* Rep.
1962–63	Cmnd.2032 xx	Registration of title to land in Scotland. Cttee. Ld. Reid, *Ch.* Rep.
1959–60	Cmnd.915 xxvii	Power of investment of trustees in Great Britain. (Govt. propose legislation to allow trustees, subject to safeguards, to invest in a wide range of fixed interest securities).
1961–62	Cmnd.1583 xxxi	Final settlement of war damage payments.

5. Private International Law

	Private International Law. Cttee. For 1st Rep. see Breviate III p. 493. Second and Third Reps. dealing with international sales of goods & with the recognition & enforcement of foreign arbitral awards, not published.
1957–58 Cmnd.491 xv	—— 4th Rep. Formal validity of wills. H. Wynn Parry, *Ch.*
1961–62 Cmnd.1515 xviii	—— 5th Rep. Recognition and enforcement of foreign arbitral awards. G. Cross, *Ch.*
1961–62 Cmnd.1648 xviii	—— 6th Rep. Draft convention on monetary law. G. Cross, *Ch.*
1962–63 Cmnd.1955 xx	—— 7th Rep. Law of domicile. G. Cross, *Ch.*

6. Administrative Tribunals

1956–57 Cmnd.218 viii	Administrative tribunals and inquiries. Cttee. O. S. Franks, *Ch.* Rep.
1956 Non-Parl.	—— Mins. of ev., 1st–21st days.
1957 Non-Parl.	—— Mins. of ev., 22nd–27th days.
1956 Non-Parl.	—— Memoranda, Vols. I–VI.
1957 Non-Parl.	—— Apps. I, II.
1957 Non-Parl.	—— Index to evidence, apps. and memoranda.
1960 Non-Parl.	Council on Tribunals. Ld. Reading, *Ch.* 1st Rep. Ld. Chancellor's Dept. (See succeeding Ann. Reps.)
1958 Non-Parl.	Procedure in connection with statutory inquiries. Memo. Dept. of Health, Scot.
1961–62 Cmnd.1787 xxiv	Position of 'third parties' at planning appeal inquiries. Council on Tribunals. Ld. Tenby, *Ch.* Rep.
1963–64 Cmnd.2471 x	Award of costs at statutory inquiries. Council on Tribunals. Ld. Tenby & D. B. Bogle, *Ch.* Rep.
1959–60 Cmnd.1033 xvii	Powers of subpoena of disciplinary tribunals. Dept. Cttee. Ld. Simonds, *Ch.* Rep.

7. Law Revision and Reform

i. England and Wales

	Law Reform. (See Breviate III, pp. 496–7).
	Law Reform. Cttee. Ld. Jenkins, *Ch.*
1956–57 Cmnd.18 xv	—— 4th Rep. Rule against perpetuities.
1956–57 Cmnd.62 xv	—— 5th Rep. Conditions and exceptions in insurance policies.
1957–58 Cmnd.310 xv	—— 6th Rep. Court power to sanction variation of trusts.
1957–58 Cmnd.501 xv	—— 7th Rep. Effect of tax liability on damages.
1958–59 Cmnd.622 xvi	—— 8th Rep. Sealing of contracts made by bodies corporate.
1960–61 Cmnd.1268 xviii	—— 9th Rep. Liability in tort between husband and wife.
1961–62 Cmnd.1782 xviii	—— 10th Rep. Innocent misrepresentation.
1962–63 Cmnd.2017 xx	—— 11th Rep. Loss of services etc.

7. Law Revision and Reform—*continued*

ii. Scotland

Law Reform Scotland. Cttee. Ld. Walker, *Ch.*

1956–57 Cmnd.88	xv	—— 1st Rep. Liability of occupiers to persons suffering injury, etc.
1956–57 Cmnd.114	xv	—— 2nd Rep. Procedure relating to actions of removal, etc.
1956–57 Cmnd.141	xv	—— 3rd Rep. Date from which interest on award of damages is to run.
1957–58 Cmnd.330	xv	—— 4th Rep. Liability of insurance companies of special conditions and of non disclosure.
1957–58 Cmnd.449	xv	—— 5th Rep. Enforcement in Scotland of orders for maintenance made by other Commonwealth Courts.
1958–59 Cmnd.635	xvi	—— 6th Rep. Assessment of damages and liability to tax.
1959–60 Cmnd.907	xvii	—— 7th Rep. The Procedure in actions in the Sheriff's Court between spouses for payment of aliment.
1959–60 Cmnd.1017	xvii	—— 8th Rep. Constitution of security over moveable property; and floating charges.
1959–60 Cmnd.1102	xvii	—— 9th Rep. Powers of trustees to sell, purchase or otherwise deal with heritable property; and the variation of trust purposes.
1960–61 Cmnd.1103	xviii	—— 10th Rep. The title of person's relatives to sue in respect of the death of that person, with particular reference to Laidlaw v. Nat. Coal Bd., 1957 S.C. 49; and the right to solatium for the death of a relative or spouse.
1962–63 Cmnd.1997	xx	—— 11th Rep. Loss of services, etc.
1963–64 Cmnd.2185	xv	—— 12th Rep. Law relating to civil liability for loss, injury and damage caused by animals.
1963–64 Cmnd.2348	xv	—— 13th Rep. The law relating to civil liability for loss, injury and damage caused by dangerous agencies escaping from land.
1963–64 Cmnd.2343	xv	—— 14th Rep. The position in relation to diligence of creditors of goods in the possession of, but not belonging to a creditor.

iii. Criminal Law Revision

Criminal Law Revision. Cttee. Ld. Sellers, *Ch.*

1958–59 Cmnd.835	xvi	—— 1st Rep. Indecency with children.
1959–60 Cmnd.1187	xvii	—— 2nd Rep. Suicide.
1962–63 Cmnd.2149	xx	—— 3rd Rep. Criminal procedure (insanity).
1962–63 Cmnd.2148	xx	—— 4th Rep. Order of closing speeches.
1963–64 Cmnd.2349	xv	—— 5th Rep. Criminal procedure (jurors).
1963–64 Cmnd.2465	xv	—— 6th Rep. Perjury and attendance of witnesses.

8. Marriage and Divorce, Illegitimacy

1955–56 Cmd.9678	xxiii	Marriage and divorce. R.Com. Ld. Morton, *Ch.* Rep.
1952	Non-Parl.	—— Mins. of ev., 1st–10th days.
1953	Non-Parl.	—— Mins. of ev., 11th–37th days.
1956	Non-Parl.	—— Mins. of ev., 38th–41st days.
1956	Non-Parl.	—— App.
1956	Non-Parl.	—— Index.

8. Marriage and Divorce, Illegitimacy—*continued*

1958–59 Cmnd.638	xvi	Matrimonial proceedings in magistrates' courts. Dept. Cttee. A. Davies, *Ch.* Rep.
1955–56 (353)	xxxvi	Consolidation of enactments relating to bastardy. Memo.

9. Sexual Offences

1955–56 (162)	xxxvi	Consolidation of enactments relating to sexual offences. Memo.
1955–56 (221–I)	vi	Sexual Offences Bill [H.L.] Jt. Sel. Cttee on Consolidation Bills. Ld. Terrington, *Ch.* 4th Rep., proc., mins. of ev.
1956–57 Cmnd.247	xiv	Homosexual offences and prostitution. Cttee. J. F. Wolfenden, *Ch.* Rep.

10. Miscellaneous Regulatory Powers

1956–57 (245)	vii	Obscene Publications Bill. Sel. Cttee. P. Spens, *Ch.* Special Rep., proc.
1957–58 (122)	vi	—— Mins. of ev., apps., index.
1957–58 (123–I)	vi	Obscene publications. Sel. Cttee. R. H. Turton, *Ch.* Rep., proc., mins. of ev., apps., index.
1955	Non-Parl.	The sale of old metals and the control of dealers in old metals. Working Party. S. J. Baker, *Ch.* Rep. apps. Home Office.
1960	Non-Parl.	Effect of draughts on the burning of portable oil heaters. Rep. D.S.I.R.

ANNEX 1. ECONOMIC AND EDUCATIONAL RELATIONS WITH COMMONWEALTH AND DEVELOPING COUNTRIES

In order to give researchers a general view of British policies in this field, the list below brings together papers dealing with the economic, technical and educational relations of Britain with the Commonwealth and developing countries generally. It does not include those dealing with the changing constitutional status of ex-colonial or other territories or with their internal policy.

1950–51 Cmd.8080	x	Colombo Plan for co-operative economic development in South and South-East Asia. Commonwealth Consultative Cttee. Rep., apps.
1951–52 Cmd.8529	ix	Colombo Plan. Consultative Cttee. 1st Ann. Rep. (See succeeding Ann. Reps.).
1956–57 Cmnd.237	xxvi	United Kingdom's role in Commonwealth development.
1957–58 Cmnd.539	x	Commonwealth trade and economic conference. Rep.
1958–59 Cmnd.786	x	Financial structure of the Colonial Development Corporation. Cttee. Ld. Sinclair, *Ch.* Rep.
1960–61 Cmnd.1449	xxvii	Commonwealth consultations on Britain's relations with the European Economic Community. Statements on talks between British ministers and other Commonwealth governments.

Commonwealth and Developing Countries—*continued*

1961–62 Cmnd.1836 xxx	Commonwealth Prime Ministers' meeting, 1962. Final communique.
1963–64 Cmnd.2441 xxv	Commonwealth Prime Ministers' meeting, 1964. Final communique.
1955–56 Cmd.9790 xxxvi	Trinidad Oil Company. Proposed purchase by the Texas Company.
1955–56 Cmd.9502 xxxvi	International Finance Corporation. Articles of agreement and explanatory memo.
1959–60 Cmnd.974 xxvii	Assistance from the United Kingdom for overseas development.
1961–62 Cmnd.1698 xxiv	Technical Co-operation. A progress report by the new Department.
1962–63 Cmnd.2147 xxxi	Aid to developing countries.
1962 Non-Parl.	Medical aid to developing countries. Working Party. A. E. Porritt, *Ch.* Rep., apps. Dept. of Technical Co-operation.
1963 Non-Parl.	Medical aid to the developing countries. Observations of H.M. Government on the Report of the Working Party. Dept. of Technical Co-operation.
1963–64 Cmnd.2286 xix	Technical assistance from Britain in agriculture, animal health, forestry and fisheries, overseas. Adv. Cttee. F. C. Bawden, *Ch.* Rep.
1963–64 Cmnd.2287 xxvi	Technical assistance for the development of natural resources overseas.
1963–64 Cmnd.2351 xix	Technical assistance for overseas geology and mining. Cttee. F. Brundrett, *Ch.* Rep.
1963–64 Cmnd.2352 xxvi	Technical assistance for overseas geology and mining. Policy on the recommendations of the committee.
1963–64 Cmnd.2433 xxvi	Research assistance for the developing countries.
1963–64 Cmnd.2257 x	Co-operatives overseas. Adv. Cttee. Ld. Peddie, *Ch.* Rep.
1963–64 Cmnd.2258 xxvi	Co-operatives overseas. Policy on the recommendations of the Advisory Committee.
1954 Non-Parl.	Reorganisation of the Colonial Service. Colonial Office.
1955–56 Cmnd.9768 xxxv	Her Majesty's Oversea Civil Service. Statement of policy regarding organisation.
1959–60 Cmnd.1193 xxvii	Service with overseas governments.
1961–62 Cmnd.1740 xxxi	Recruitment for service overseas. Future policy.
1962 Non-Parl.	Public service commission in overseas territories. J. A. Mulhall. Notes for the guidance of members of commissions. Dept. of Technical Co-operation.
1963 Non-Parl.	Training in public administration for overseas countries. Cttee. Ld. Bridges, *Ch.* Rep., apps., index. Dept. of Technical Co-operation.

Commonwealth and Developing Countries—*continued*

1962–63	Cmnd.2099 xxxi	Training in public administration for overseas countries. Policy on the recommendations of the committee.
1955	Non-Parl.	Provision of agricultural education of university degree standard in British Caribbean territories. R. S. Wood. Rep. Colonial Office.
1955–56	Cmd.9515 xiv	Higher education overseas, 1946–54. Inter-University Council. A. Carr-Saunders, *Ch.* Rep. and Review.
1958–59	Cmnd.841 xi	Commonwealth education. Conference. P. R. Morris, *Ch.* Rep.
1959–60	Cmnd.894 xxvii	Commonwealth scholarship and fellowship plan. Proposed arrangements for the administration of the plan in the U.K.
1959–60	Cmnd.1032 xxvii	Commonwealth educational co-operation.
1961–62	Cmnd.1541 xi	Commonwealth Scholarship Com. 1st Ann. Rep. (See succeeding Ann. Reps.).
1960–61	Cmnd.1255 xviii	Legal education for students from Africa. Cttee. Ld. Denning, *Ch.* Rep.
1961–62	Cmnd.1655 xi	Commonwealth education. 2nd Conference. K. L. Shrimali, *Ch.* Rep.

ANNEX 2. DEFENCE POLICY AND THE ECONOMY

This volume does not include papers concerned with military and naval policy, or with the organisation and operation of the armed forces, but decisions on these matters have repercussions on the economy in the field of manpower supply, industrial production, finance, etc. A brief list of papers having some bearing on these matters is given below.

1954–55	Cmd.9433 iv	Organisation and administration of boys' units in the army. Cttee. Rep.
1955	Non-Parl.	Effects of national service on the education and employment of young men. Enquiry. Rep., app. Min. of Labour & N.S.
1955–56	Cmd.9523 x	Territorial army. Cttee. F. H. Maclean, *Ch.* Rep.
1955–56	Cmd.9608 xxxii	National service. White Paper.
1955–56	Cmd.9676 xxxvi	Export of surplus war material.
1955–56	Cmd.9692 xxxii	Service pay and pensions.
1956–57	Cmnd.35 xvii	Employment of national service men in the U.K. Cttee. Rep.
1956–57	Cmnd.124 xxiii	Defence: outline of future policy.
1956–57	Cmnd.175 xxiii	Call up of men to the forces, 1957–60.
1956–57	Cmnd.230 xxii	Future organisation of the army.
1956–57	Cmnd.231 xxiii	Compensation for premature retirement from the armed forces.

Defence Policy and the Economy—*continued*

1957–58	Cmnd.363	xxi	Defence. Rep. Britain's contribution to peace and security.
1957–58	Cmnd.476	xxi	Central organisation for defence.
1958–59	Cmnd.545	viii	Recruiting. Adv. Cttee. P. J. Grigg, *Ch*. Rep.
1958–59	Cmnd.570	xxii	Recruiting. The government's comments on the Report of the Advisory Committee.
1958–59	Cmnd.662	xxii	Defence. Rep. Progress of the five-year defence plan.
1958–59	Cmnd.789	viii	Resettlement Advisory Board. F. C. Hooper, *Ch*. Progress Rep. 1957–9.
1959–60	Cmnd.952	xxiv	Defence, 1960. Rep.
1960–61	Cmnd.1288	xxiv	Defence, 1961. Rep.
1961–62	Cmnd.1639	xxvii	Defence, 1962. Statement. The next five years.
1961–62	Cmnd.1666	xxvii	Service pay and pensions.
1962–63	Cmnd.1936	xxvii	Defence, 1963. Statement.
1962–63	Cmnd.2097	xxvii	Central organisation for defence.
1963–64	Cmnd.2270	xxii	Defence, 1964. Statement.
1964–65	Cmnd.2592	xxv	Defence estimates, 1965. Statement.
1956	Non-Parl.		Forces medical and dental services. Cttee. Ld. Waverley, *Ch*. Rep. Min. of Defence.
1956	Non-Parl.		—— 2nd Rep.
1957–58	Cmnd.352	xxiv	Replacement of certain emergency legislation by the Land Powers (Defence) Bill.
1958–59	Cmnd.568	xxii	Armed Forces (Housing Loans). Memo. on the proposed resolution.
1955–56	Cmd.9788	xiv	Defence contracts. [Power of the Crown to authorise the use of unpatented inventions, etc., in defence contracts]. Cttee. H. G. Howitt, *Ch*. Rep.
1963–64	Cmnd.2428	xvi	Pricing of Ministry of Aviation contracts. Inquiry. J. G. Lang, *Ch*. 1st Rep.
1964–65	Cmnd.2581	xix	—— 2nd Rep.

APPENDIX I

SELECT LIST OF ANNUAL REPORTS 1955-1964

The annual reports of departments and other statutory bodies, and the memoranda and statistics they contain, are invaluable sources of information. The references to all those issued in the sessional papers during this period are given in the decennial 'General Alphabetical Index . . . 1950 to 1958–59', and in the sessional indexes thereafter, but for the convenience of readers the references to some of the principal series are given below.

The first issue of a number of important new annual reports has been included in the appropriate sections of the main body of the work, giving either the session (for Parliamentary Papers) or year of publication (for Non-Parliamentary publications). The sessional indexes or H.M.S.O. annual *Catalogues* should be consulted for details of subsequent reports which have not been included in this Appendix.

The H.M.S.O. annual *Catalogues* should also be consulted for details of annual reports, formerly issued as sessional papers, which in this period have either become Non-Parliamentary publications, have been discontinued, merged with or replaced by other annuals differently titled.

The list below gives the full titles of the principal series relating to the main subjects covered by the Select List and notes any changes. The lists of references give session, paper number, sessional volume number and the year covered by the report concerned.

1. Finance. Finance accounts of the U.K.
2. Inland Revenue. Reports of the Commissioners of H.M. Inland Revenue.

3. Customs. Reports of the Commissioners of H.M. Customs and Excise.
4. Economic Survey. Replaced in 1963 by the Economic Report, issued as a Supplement to the March issue of *Economic Trends*.

5. National Income. Preliminary estimates of National Income and Expenditure. 1962–63: Preliminary Estimates of National Income and Balance of Payments. See also quarterly figures in *Economic Trends*, from January, 1957.
6. Balance of Payments. U.K. Balance of Payments. Replaced in March, 1963, by quarterly figures in *Economic Trends*. See also Preliminary Estimates of National Income and Balance of Payments, 1962–63 onwards.

7. Bank of England. Reports. (Report for 1959–60 published by Bank of England. Reports for 1960–61 onwards; Non-Parl. Treasury.)
8. Coal. National Coal Board. Annual Reports and Statements of Accounts. 1955–56: Vol. I, Report. Vol. II, Accounts and Statistical Tables.

9. Gas. Gas Council. Reports and Statements of Accounts.
10. Electricity. British Electricity Authority. Reports and Statements of Accounts. 1955–56: Central Electricity Authority. 1958–59: Electricity Council.

11. C.E.G.B. Central Electricity Generating Board. Reports and Accounts.
12. Atomic Energy. U.K. Atomic Energy Authority. Annual Reports.

13. Transport. British Transport Commission. Annual Reports, Statements of Accounts and Statistics. Vol. I, Report. Vol. II, Financial and Statistical Accounts. (The Commission was dissolved by the Transport Act, 1962. Was succeeded by five separate bodies—British Railways Board, British Transport Docks Board, British Waterways Board, London Transport Board and Transport Holding Company, each of which issued its first annual report in session 1963–64.)
14. Labour. Ministry of Labour and National Service. Reports. 1959–60: Ministry of Labour.

15. Factories. Chief Inspector of Factories. Annual Reports.
16. Industrial Health. Chief Inspector of Factories. Annual Reports on Industrial Health.

17. National Assistance. National Assistance Board. Reports.
18. National Insurance. Ministry of Pensions and National Insurance. Reports.

19. Health. Ministry of Health. Reports.
20. Health, Chief M.O. Ministry of Health. Annual Reports of the Chief Medical Officer on the State of the Public Health (1963 onwards: Non-Parliamentary).

Select List of Annual Reports—*continued*

21. Health (Scotland). Reports of the Department of Health for Scotland and of the Scottish Health Services Council. 1956–57: Reports of the Department of Health for Scotland. (The Report of the Council became Non-Parl. in 1957.). 1960–61: Report, Pt. I, Health and Welfare Services. Pt. II, Housing, Planning and Environment. 1962–63: Pt. I continued by Reports of Scottish Home and Health Department. Pt. II continued by Reports of Scottish Development Department.
22. Housing. Ministry of Housing and Local Government. Reports.

23. Education. Ministry of Education. Reports and Statistics of Public Education for England and Wales. 1961–62: Ministry of Education. Reports. (Statistics of Education, 1961 onwards Non-Parl.).
24. Education (Scotland). Reports of the Secretary of State for Scotland.

25. Civil Judicial Statistics, England and Wales.
26. Civil Judicial Stats. (Scot.). Civil Judicial Statistics, Scotland.

27. Criminal Statistics. Statistics relating to Crime and Criminal Proceedings (England and Wales).
28. Criminal Statistics, Scotland. Statistics relating to police apprehensions and criminal proceedings.

29. Prisons. Commissioners of Prisons. Reports. 1963–64: Prisons and Borstals. Reports on the work of the Prison Department. (Statistical Tables published separately from Report, usually in subsequent session; e.g. Tables for 1962 and 1963; 1963–64 Cmnd.2314, xviii. 1964–65 Cmnd.2630, xxii.)
30. Prisons (Scot.). Reports on Prisons in Scotland.

1–2

Session	Finance		for the year	Inland Revenue		for the year
1955–56	(303)	xxix	1955/6	Cmd.9667	xxi	1954/5
1956–57	(204)	xx	1956/7	Cmnd.54	xiv	1955/6
1957–58	(217)	xix	1957/8	Cmnd.341	xv	1956/7
1958–59	(221)	xx	1958/9	Cmnd.628	xvi	1957/8
1959–60	(229)	xxii	1959/60	Cmnd.922	xvii	1958/9
1960–61	(231)	xxii	1960/1	Cmnd.1258	xviii	1959/60
1961–62	(217)	xxv	1961/2	Cmnd.1598	xvii	1960/1
1962–63	(248)	xxvi	1962/3	Cmnd.1906	xx	1961/2
1963–64	(235)	xxi	1963/4	Cmnd.2283	xv	1962/3
1964–65	(231)	xxiv	1964/5	Cmnd.2572	xviii	1963/4

3–4

Session	Customs		for the year	Economic Survey		for the year
1955–56	Cmd.9675	xiv	1954/5	Cmd.9728	xxxvi	1956
1956–57	Cmnd.69	x	1955/6	Cmnd.113	xxvi	1957
1957–58	Cmnd.344	x	1956/7	Cmnd.394	xxiv	1958
1958–59	Cmnd.613	xi	1957/8	Cmnd.708	xxv	1959
1959–60	Cmnd.912	xii	1958/9	Cmnd.976	xxvii	1960
1960–61	Cmnd.1234	xiii	1959/60	Cmnd.1334	xxvii	1961
1961–62	Cmnd.1566	xii	1960/1	Cmnd.1678	xxxi	1962
1962–63	Cmnd.1933	xi	1961/2			
1963–64	Cmnd.2216	x	1962/3			
1964–65	Cmnd.2539	xiii	1963/4			

Select List of Annual Reports—*continued*

5–6

Session	National Income		for the years	Balance of Payments		for the years
1955–56	Cmd.9729	xxix	1950/5	Cmd.9585	xxix	1946/55
				Cmd.9731	xxix	1946/55
				Cmd.9871	xxix	1946/56
1956–57	Cmnd.123	xx	1951/6	Cmnd.122	xx	1946/56
				Cmnd.273	xx	1954/7
1957–58	Cmnd.398	xix	1952/7	Cmnd.399	xix	1955/7
				Cmnd.540	xix	1955/8
1958–59	Cmnd.712	xx	1953/8	Cmnd.700	xx	1956/8
1959–60	Cmnd.988	xxii	1954/9	Cmnd.861	xxii	1956/9
				Cmnd.977	xxii	1957/9
				Cmnd.1188	xxii	1957/60
1960–61	Cmnd.1333	xxii	1955/60	Cmnd.1329	xxii	1958/60
				Cmnd.1506	xxii	1958/61
1961–62	Cmnd.1679	xxv	1956/61	Cmnd.1671	xxv	1959/61
				Cmnd.1837	xxv	1959/62
1962–63	Cmnd.1984	xxvi	1957/62			
1963–64	Cmnd.2328	xxi	1958/63			
1964–65	Cmnd.2629	xxiv	1959/64			

7–8

Session	Bank of England		for the year	Coal		for the year
1955–56	Cmd.9541	xi	1954/5	(1)	xii	1954
	Cmd.9828	xi	1955/6	(263–I) (263–II)	xii	1955
1956–57	Cmnd.240	viii	1956/7	(176–I) (176–II)	ix	1956
1957–58	Cmnd.500	viii	1957/8	(180) (181)	viii	1957
1958–59	Cmnd.801	ix	1958/9	(158) (159)	ix	1958
1959–60	Continuing Non-Parl.			(191) (192)	ix	1959
1960–61				(195) (196)	ix	1960
1961–62				(189) (190)	x	1961
1962–63				(213) (214)	ix	1962
1963–64				(317) (318)	x	Jan.'63–Mar.'64
1964–65				(314) (315)	xii	1964/5

9–10

Session	Gas		for the year	Electricity		for the year
1955–56	(86)	xviii	1954/5	(72)	xv	1954/5
	(393)	xix	1955/6	(367)	xvi	1955/6
1956–57	(285)	xii	1956/7	(257)	xi	1956/7
1957–58	(302)	xiii	1957/8	(288)	xi	1957/8
1958–59	(298)	xiv	1958/9	(312)	xii	1958/9
1959–60	(330)	xv	1959/60	(315)	xiii	1959/60
1960–61	(319)	xvi	1960/1	(304)	xiv	1960/1
1961–62	(307)	xvi	1961/2	(292)	xiii	1961/2
1962–63	(332)	xviii	1962/3	(317)	xv	1962/3
1963–64	(346)	xiii	1963/4	(331)	xi	1963/4
1964–65	(343)	xvi	1964/5	(328)	xiii	1964/5

Select List of Annual Reports—*continued*

11–12

Session	C.E.G.B.		for the year	Atomic Energy		for the year
1955–56				(95)	xi	1954/5
				(323)	xi	1955/6
1956–57				(219)	viii	1956/7
1957–58				(242)	vii	1957/8
1958–59	(313)	xii	1958/9	(249)	viii	1958/9
1959–60	(316)	xiii	1959/60	(243)	ix	1959/60
1960–61	(305)	xiv	1960/1	(229)	ix	1960/1
1961–62	(293)	xiii	1961/2	(221)	viii	1961/2
1962–63	(318)	xv	1962/3	(252)	viii	1962/3
1963–64	(332)	xi	1963/4	(246)	viii	1963/4
1964–65	(329)	xiii	1964/5	(311)	xi	1964/5

13–14

Session	Transport			for the year	Labour		for the year
1955–56	(20–I) (20–II)		xxviii	1954	Cmd.9522	xxii	1954
	(290–I) (290–II)		xxviii	1955	Cmd.9791	xxii	1955
1956–57	(187–I) (187–II)		xix	1956	Cmnd.242	xv	1956
1957–58	(215–I) (215–II)		xviii	1957	Cmnd.468	xv	1957
1958–59	(216) (216–I)		xix	1958	Cmnd.745	xvi	1958
1959–60	(226) (226–I)		xxi	1959	Cmnd.1059	xvii	1959
1960–61	(213) (213–I)		xxi	1960	Cmnd.1364	xviii	1960
1961–62	(209) (209–I)		xxiv	1961			
1962–63	(232) (232–I)		xxv	1962			
1963–64							
1964–65							

15–16

Session	Factories		for the year	Industrial Health		for the year
1955–56	Cmd.9605	xvii	1954			
1956–57	Cmnd.8	xii	1955			
1957–58	Cmnd.329	xii	1956			
	Cmnd.521	xii	1957			
1958–59	Cmnd.810	xiii	1958	Cmnd.558	xiii	1957
				Cmnd.811	xiii	1958
1959–60	Cmnd.1107	xiv	1959	Cmnd.1137	xiv	1959
1960–61	Cmnd.1479	xv	1960	Cmnd.1478	xv	1960
1961–62	Cmnd.1816	xv	1961	Cmnd.1815	xv	1961
1962–63	Cmnd.2128	xvii	1962	Cmnd.2129	xvii	1962
1963–64	Cmnd.2450	xiii	1963	Cmnd.2444	xiii	1963
1964–65	Cmnd.2724	xv	1964	Cmnd.2723	xv	1964

17–18

Session	National Assistance		for the year	National Insurance		for the year
1955–56	Cmd.9530	xi	1954	Cmd.9495	xxvi	1954
	Cmd.9781	xi	1955	Cmd.9826	xxvi	1955
1956–57	Cmnd.181	viii	1956	Cmnd.229	xviii	1956

Select List of Annual Reports—*continued*

Session	National Assistance		for the year	National Insurance		for the year
1957–58	Cmnd.444	vii	1957	Cmnd.493	xvii	1957
1958–59	Cmnd.781	viii	1958	Cmnd.826	xviii	1958
1959–60	Cmnd.1085	ix	1959	Cmnd.1133	xx	1959
1960–61	Cmnd.1410	viii	1960	Cmnd.1458	xx	1960
1961–62	Cmnd.1730	viii	1961	Cmnd.1764	xx	1961
1962–63	Cmnd.2078	viii	1962	Cmnd.2069	xxiii	1962
1963–64	Cmnd.2386	viii	1963	Cmnd.2392	xviii	1963
1964–65	Cmnd.2674	xi	1964	Cmnd.2686	xxi	1964

19–20

Session	Health		for the year	Health, Chief M.O.		for the year
1955–56	Cmd.9566	xx	1954	Cmd.9627	xx	1954
	Cmd.9857	xx	1955			
1956–57				Cmnd.16	xiii	1955
1957–58	Cmnd.293	xiv	1956	Cmnd.325	xiv	1956
	Cmnd.495	xiv	1957			
1958–59	Cmnd.806	xv	1958	Cmnd.559	xv	1957
1959–60	Cmnd.1086	xvi	1959	Cmnd.871	xvi	1958
1960–61	Cmnd.1418	xvii	1960	Cmnd.1207	xvii	1959
1961–62	Cmnd.1754	xvii	1961	Cmnd.1550	xvii	1960
1962–63	Cmnd.2062	xix	1962	Cmnd.1856	xix	1961
1963–64	Cmnd.2389	xv	1963	Continuing		
1964–65	Cmnd.2688	xvii	1964	Non-Parl.		

21–22

Session	Health (Scotland)		for the year	Housing		for the year
1955–56	Cmd.9742	xxi	1955	Cmd.9559	xxi	1950/1 –1954
				Cmd.9876	xxi	1955
1956–57	Cmnd.140	xiii	1956	Cmnd.193	xiv	1956
1957–58	Cmnd.385	xiv	1957	Cmnd.419	xiv	1957
1958–59	Cmnd.697	xv	1958	Cmnd.737	xv	1958
1959–60	Cmnd.983	xvi	1959	Cmnd.1027	xvi	1959
1960–61	Cmnd.1320	xvii	1960	Cmnd.1435	xvii	1960
	Cmnd.1361	xvii	1960			
1961–62	Cmnd.1703	xvii	1961	Cmnd.1725	xvii	1961
	Cmnd.1652	xvii	1961			
1962–63	Cmnd.1996	xix	1962	Cmnd.1976	xix	1962
1963–64	Cmnd.2359	xv	1963	Cmnd.2338	xv	1963
1964–65	Cmnd.2700	xvii	1964	Cmnd.2668	xvii	1964

23–24

Session	Education		for the year	Education (Scotland)		for the year
1955–56	Cmd.9521	xiv	1954	Cmd.9722	xiv	1955
	Cmd.9785	xiv	1955			
1956–57	Cmnd.223	x	1956	Cmnd.162	x	1956
1957–58	Cmnd.454	x	1957	Cmnd.407	x	1957
1958–59	Cmnd.777	xi	1958	Cmnd.740	xi	1958

Select List of Annual Reports—*continued*

Session	Education		*for the* *year*	Education (Scotland)		*for the* *year*
1959–60	Cmnd.1088	xii	1959	Cmnd.1018	xii	1959
1960–61	Cmnd.1439	xiii	1960	Cmnd.1359	xiii	1960
1961–62	Cmnd.1737	xiii	1961	Cmnd.1673	xiii	1961
1962–63	Cmnd.1990	xi	1962	Cmnd.1975	xv	1962
1963–64	Cmnd.2316	xi	1963	Cmnd.2307	xi	1963
1964–65	Cmnd.2612	xiii	1964	Cmnd.2600	xiii	1964

25–26

Session	Civil Judicial Statistics		*for the* *year*	Civil Judicial Stats. (Scot.)		*for the* *year*
1955–56	Cmd.9505	xxxv	1954	Cmd.9513	xxxv	1954
	Cmd.9775	xxxv	1955	Cmd.9808	xxxv	1955
1956–57	Cmnd.224	xxvi	1956	Cmnd.215	xxvi	1956
1957–58	Cmnd.434	xxiv	1957	Cmnd.478	xxiv	1957
1958–59	Cmnd.802	xxv	1958			
1959–60	Cmnd.1126	xxvii	1959	Cmnd.850	xxvii	1958
				Cmnd.1047	xxvii	1959
1960–61	Cmnd.1416	xxvii	1960	Cmnd.1408	xxvii	1960
1961–62	Cmnd.1745	xxx	1961	Cmnd.1744	xxx	1961
1962–63	Cmnd.2055	xxx	1962	Cmnd.2076	xxx	1962
1963–64	Cmnd.2384	xxv	1963	Cmnd.2373	xxv	1963
1964–65	Cmnd.2666	xxviii	1964	Cmnd.2701	xxviii	1964

27–28

Session	Criminal Statistics		*for the* *year*	Criminal Statistics (Scot.)		*for the* *year*
1955–56	Cmd.9574	xxxv	1954	Cmd.9750	xxxv	1955
	Cmd.9884	xxxv	1955			
1956–57				Cmnd.157	xxvi	1956
1957–58	Cmnd.286	xxiv	1956	Cmnd.426	xxiv	1957
	Cmnd.529	xxiv	1957			
1958–59	Cmnd.803	xxv	1958	Cmnd.746	xxv	1958
1959–60	Cmnd.1100	xxvii	1959	Cmnd.1024	xxvii	1959
1960–61	Cmnd.1437	xxvii	1960	Cmnd.1343	xxvii	1960
1961–62	Cmnd.1779	xxx	1961	Cmnd.1702	xxx	1961
1962–63	Cmnd.2120	xxx	1962	Cmnd.2011	xxx	1962
1963–64				Cmnd.2344	xxv	1963
1964–65	Cmnd.2525	xxviii	1963	Cmnd.2702	xxviii	1964

29–30

Session	Prisons		*for the* *year*	Prisons (Scot.)		*for the* *year*
1955–56	Cmd.9547	xxvii	1954	Cmd.9760	xxvii	1955
1956–57	Cmnd.10	xviii	1955	Cmnd.164	xviii	1956
1957–58	Cmnd.322	xvii	1956	Cmnd.429	xvii	1957
	Cmnd.496	xvii	1957			
1958–59	Cmnd.825	xviii	1958	Cmnd.765	xviii	1958
1959–60	Cmnd.1117	xx	1959	Cmnd.1048	xx	1959
1960–61	Cmnd.1467	xx	1960	Cmnd.1383	xx	1960

Sessions	Prisons		for the year	Prisons (Scot.)		for the year
1961–62	Cmnd.1798	xxiii	1961	Cmnd.1722	xxiii	1961
1962–63	Cmnd.2030	xxiii	1962	Cmnd.2143	xxiii	1962
1963–64	Cmnd.2381	xviii	1963	Cmnd.2367	xviii	1963
1964–65	Cmnd.2708	xxii	1964	Cmnd.2703	xxii	1964

APPENDIX II

SELECT LIST OF RESEARCH SERIES AND ESTIMATES COMMITTEE REPORTS

During the period covered by this book a number of new series of research reports were published as Non-Parliamentary publications; reports in other series of long standing also appeared. The H.M.S.O. annual *Catalogues* and Sectional Lists should be consulted for full details of these and other series, but it is hoped that the brief lists below will give some indication of the range of topics with which various government departments and their research units have been concerned during the period under review.

Guides to Official Sources   General Register Office

1. Labour statistics. rev. ed.; 1958
2. Census reports of Great Britain, 1801–1931; 1951
3. Local government statistics; 1953
4. Agricultural and food statistics; 1958
5. Social security statistics; 1961
6. Census of production reports; 1961

Studies in Official Statistics

3. National income statistics. Sources and methods; 1956   C.S.O.
4. Length of working life of males in Great Britain; 1959   Min. of Labour & N.S.
5. New contributions to economic statistics; 1959   C.S.O.
6. Method of construction and calculation of the index of retail prices. 2nd ed.; 1959 Min. of Labour & N.S. 3rd ed.; 1964
7. Index of industrial production: methods of compilation; 1960   C.S.O.
8. Input-output tables for the U.K., 1954; 1961   C.S.O.
9. New contributions to economic statistics. 2nd series; 1962   C.S.O.
10. New contributions to economic statistics. 3rd series; 1964   C.S.O.

Manpower Studies   Min. of Labour

1. The pattern of the future; 1964
2. The metal industries; 1965
3. The construction industry; 1965
4. Computers in offices; 1965

Problems of Progress in Industry   D.S.I.R.

1. Men, steel and technical change; 1957
2. Managers for tomorrow; 1957
3. Management and technology; 1958
4. What they read and why: use of technical literature in the electrical and electronics industries; 1959
5. Human problems in innovation; 1960

Research Series and Estimates Committee Reports—*continued*

6. Training made easier. Review of four recent studies; 1960
7. The older worker and his job; 1960
8. Ergonomics of automation; 1960
9. Automation and skill; 1960
10. Woman, wife and worker; 1960
11. Money for effort; 1961
12. Human sciences. Aid to industry; 1961
13. The supervisor and his job; 1963
14. Teaching machines and their use in industry; 1963
15. Training the adult worker; 1964
16. How research can help training; 1964
17. Subjective standards in industrial inspection; 1964
18. Work flow in batch production; 1966

Studies on Medical and Population Subjects   General Register Office

9. General practitioners' records. Analysis of the clinical records of some general practices during the period April, 1952 to March, 1954; 1956
10. Tuberculosis statistics for England and Wales, 1938 to 1955. An analysis of trends and geographical distribution; 1957
11. Internal migration. Study of the frequency of movements of migrants; 1957
12. Survey of sickness, 1943 to 1952; 1958
13. Cancer statistics for England and Wales, 1901–1955. Summary of data relating to mortality and morbidity; 1958
14. Morbidity statistics from general practice. Vol.I, General. Vol.II, Occupation. Vol.III, Disease in general practice; 1958, 1960, 1962
15. Social and biological factors in infant mortality; 1959
16. Area of residence of mental hospital patients. Admissions to mental hospitals in England and Wales in 1957, according to area of residence, diagnosis, sex and age; 1960
17. Mass miniature radiography. Report on three years' examinations in England and Wales, 1955–57; 1961
18. A cohort study of patients first admitted to mental hospitals in 1954 and 1955; 1963

Reports on Public Health and Medical Subjects   Min. of Health

96. Outbreak of food poisoning due to Salmonella bovis morbificans (Basenau) in which the vehicle of infection was meat pies; 1955
97. Report on confidential enquiries into maternal deaths in England and Wales, 1952–54; 1957
98. Survey of services available to the chronic sick and elderly, 1954–1955; 1957
99. Standards of normal weight in infancy; 1959
100. Influenza epidemic in England and Wales, 1957–1958; 1960
101. Rubella and other virus infections during pregnancy; 1960
102. Developmental progress of infants and young children; 1960
103. Report on confidential enquiries into maternal deaths in England and Wales, 1955 to 1957; 1960
104. Leucotomy in England and Wales, 1942–1954; 1961
105. The conduct of the fluoridation studies in the U.K. and the results achieved after five years; 1962
106. University Grants Committee. Postgraduate medical education and the specialties. With special reference to the problem in London; 1962
107. Report on the outbreak of poliomyelitis during 1961 in Kingston-upon-Hull and the East Riding of Yorkshire; 1963
108. Report on confidential enquiries into maternal deaths in England and Wales, 1958–1960; 1963
109. Smallpox 1961–62; 1963

Research Series and Estimates Committee Reports—*continued*
110. Recent N.H.S. prescribing trends; 1964
111. Requirements of man for protein; 1964
112. Deformities caused by thalidomide; 1964

Studies in the Causes of Delinquency and the Treatment of Offenders   Home Office

1. Prediction methods in relation to Borstal training; 1955
2. Time spent awaiting trial; 1960
3. Delinquent generations; 1961
4. Murder; 1961
5. Persistent criminals. A study of all offenders liable to preventive detention in 1956; 1963

Estimates Committee. Reports of the Estimates Committee often contain valuable information not readily available elsewhere. The decennial 'General Alphabetical Index . . . 1950 to 1958–59' and the sessional indexes thereafter should be consulted for the full list of reports. Listed below are those reports, with the departmental replies, which relate to the subject areas covered by the main part of this book. As far as possible they have been listed in an order which corresponds with the main subject classification.

1960–61 (168)	v	House of Commons library. Rep., mins. of ev., apps.
(246)	vi	—— Dept. reply.
1960–61 (241)	v	Ministry of Agriculture, Fisheries & Food. Rep., mins. of ev., apps.
1961–62 (47)	v	—— Dept. reply.
1962–63 (17)	v	—— Dept. reply.
1959–60 (260)	vi	Colonial Office. Rep., mins. of ev., app.
1960–61 (26)	iv	—— Dept. reply.
1958–59 (252)	v	Commonwealth Relations Office. Rep., mins. of ev., apps.
1959–60 (250)	v	—— Dept. reply.
1956–57 (182)	vi	Customs & Excise. Rep., mins. of ev.
(307)	vi	—— Dept. reply.
1959–60 (290)	vi	—— Dept. reply.
1962–63 (293)	vi	Home Office. Rep., mins. of ev., apps.
1963–64 (12)	v	—— Dept. reply.
1959–60 (259)	v	Central Office of Information. Rep., mins. of ev., apps.
1960–61 (129)	v	—— Dept. reply.
1960–61 (245)	vi	Board of Inland Revenue. Rep., mins. of ev., apps.
1961–62 (18)	v	—— Dept. reply.
1962–63 (240)	v	—— Dept. reply.
1956–57 (199)	vi	Meteorological services and Royal Greenwich Observatory. Rep., mins. of ev., apps.
1957–58 (263)	v	—— Dept. reply.
1962–63 (239)	v	Ordnance Survey. Rep., mins. of ev., apps.
1963–64 (124)	v	—— Dept. reply.
1957–58 (198)	iv	Ministry of Power. Rep., mins. of ev., app.
1958–59 (22)	iv	—— Dept. reply.
1957–58 (245)	v	Department of Scientific & Industrial Research. Rep., mins. of ev., apps.
1958–59 (224)	iv	—— Dept. reply.
1959–60 (172)	v	—— Dept. reply.

Research Series and Estimates Committee Reports—*continued*

1956–57 (33)	v	H.M. Stationery Office. Rep., mins. of ev., apps.
(198)	vi	—— Dept. reply.
1963–64 (303)	vi	Department of Technical Co-operation. Rep., mins. of ev., apps.
1964–65 (89)	vi	—— Dept. reply.
1959–60 (258)	v	Board of Trade. Rep., mins. of ev., apps.
1960–61 (30)	iv	—— Dept. reply.
1961–62 (241)	vi	War Office. Rep., mins. of ev., apps.
1962–63 (25)	v	—— Dept. reply.
1955–56 (234)	viii	Ministry of Works: Directorate General of Works. Rep., mins. of ev., apps.
1956–57 (102)	v	—— Dept. reply.
1962–63 (294)	vi	Downing Street and Old Treasury Buildings and State House, Holborn. Rep., mins. of ev., apps.
1963–64 (273)	v	—— Dept. reply.
1957–58 (254–I)	v	Treasury control of expenditure. Rep., proc., mins. of ev., apps.
1958–59 (227)	iv	—— Dept. reply.
1963–64 (228)	v	Treasury control of establishments. Rep., mins. of ev., apps.
(297)	vi	—— Dept. reply.
1954–55 (130)	iii	National Savings Committee. Rep., proc., mins. of ev., app.
1955–56 (111)	vii	—— Dept. reply.
1961–62 (77)	v	Agricultural and food grants and subsidies. Rep., mins. of ev., apps.
1963–64 (272)	v	Forestry Commission. Rep., mins. of ev., apps.
1964–65 (199)	vi	—— Dept. reply.
1955–56 (139)	vii	Development areas. Rep., mins. of ev., apps.
1956–57 (135)	v	—— Dept. reply.
1962–63 (229)	v	Administration of the Local Employment Act, 1960. Rep., mins. of ev., apps.
1963–64 (34)	v	—— Dept. reply.
1961–62 (191)	v	Assistance to the cotton industry. Rep., mins. of ev., apps.
1958–59 (316–I)	v	U.K. Atomic Energy Authority. Rep., mins. of ev., apps.
1959–60 (80)	v	—— Dept. reply.
1958–59 (223)	iv	Trunk roads. Rep., mins. of ev., apps.
1959–60 (172)	v	—— Dept. reply.
1961–62 (227)	vi	Classified roads. Rep., mins. of ev., apps.
1962–63 (100)	v	—— Dept. reply.
1955–56 (128)	vii	Civil aerodromes and ground services. Rep., mins. of ev., apps.
1956–57 (35)	v	—— Dept. reply.
1960–61 (233)	v	London's airports. Rep., mins. of ev., apps.
1961–62 (46)	v	—— Dept. reply.

Research Series and Estimates Committee Reports—*continued*

1963–64 (42)	v	Transport aircraft. Rep., mins. of ev., apps.
(241)	v	—— Dept. reply.
1956–57 (240)	vi	Youth employment service and youth service grants. Rep., mins. of ev., apps.
1957–58 (66)	iv	—— Dept. reply.
1956–57 (222)	vi	Running costs of hospitals. Rep., mins. of ev., apps.
1957–58 (129)	iv	—— Dept. reply.
1958–59 (124)	iv	—— Dept. reply.
1962–63 (40)	v	Dental services. Rep., mins. of ev., apps.
(267)	vi	—— Dept. reply.
1957–58 (255)	v	Nature Conservancy. Rep., mins. of ev., app.
1959–60 (172)	v	—— Dept. reply.
1959–60 (274)	vi	Historic buildings and ancient monuments. Rep., mins. of ev.
1960–61 (91)	iv	—— Dept. reply.
1960–61 (284)	vi	School building. Rep., mins. of ev., apps.
1961–62 (17)	v	—— Dept. reply.
1955–56 (209)	viii	Legal aid. Rep., mins. of ev., apps.
(346)	viii	—— Dept. reply.
1957–58 (30)	iv	Police (England & Wales). Rep., mins. of ev., apps.
(264)	v	—— Dept. reply.
1958–59 (22)	iv	—— Dept. reply.
1955–56 (198)	vii	Works and buildings of the Service Departments (Army). Rep., mins. of ev., apps.
1956–57 (102)	v	—— Dept. reply.
1955–56 (322)	viii	Food supplies of the armed services. Rep., mins. of ev., apps.
1957–58 (31)	iv	—— Dept.reply.
1955–56 (345)	viii	Naval research and development. Rep., mins. of ev., apps.
1956–57 (307)	vi	—— Dept. reply.
1956–57 (34)	v	Supply of military aircraft. Rep., mins. of ev., app.
(34–Ind.)	v	—— Index.
(307)	v	—— Dept. reply.
1957–58 (238)	v	Land Branches of the Service Departments. Rep., mins. of ev., apps.
1958–59 (123)	iv	—— Dept. reply.
1958–59 (253)	v	Medical services of the armed forces. Rep., mins. of ev., apps.
1959–60 (291)	vi	—— Dept. reply.
1961–62 (49)	v	Trooping. Rep., mins. of ev., apps.
(196)	v	—— Dept. reply.
1961–62 (263)	vi	Her Majesty's dockyards. Rep., mins. of ev., apps.
1962–63 (101)	v	—— Dept. reply.
1962–63 (282)	vi	Military expenditure overseas. Rep., mins. of ev., apps.
1963–64 (123)	v	—— Dept. reply.
(302)	vi	—— Rep., mins. of ev., apps.
1964–65 (55)	vi	—— Dept. reply.
1963–64 (296)	vi	Service colleges. Rep., mins. of ev., apps.
1964–65 (88)	vi	—— Dept. reply.

ALPHABETICAL SUBJECT INDEX

This brief index is designed to assist readers to find individual papers. It is based on the key word or words of the title. Where this is identical with the main subject heading, no separate entry has been made.

CHAIRMAN AND AUTHOR INDEX

This index is intended as a guide to finding papers by the name of the chairman or author as printed on them. It does not necessarily identify persons, since there may be change of surname, elevation to the peerage under a different name, or change of individual's practice in signature respecting initials and hyphens. Sometimes individuals may be popularly known by both Christian and surname together: readers should then consult the index under both.